Conserving America?

Conserving America?

Essays on Present Discontents

Patrick J. Deneen

Dissident American Thought Today Series

ST. AUGUSTINE'S PRESS
South Bend, Indiana

Manufactured in the United States of America.

2 3 4 5 6   23 22 21 20 19 18 17

Library of Congress Cataloging in Publication Data
Deneen, Patrick J., 1964- author.
Conserving America?: essays on present discontents /
Patrick J. Deneen.
South Bend, Indiana: St. Augustine's Press, 2016.
Series: Dissident American thought today series
Includes index.
LCCN 2016012556
ISBN 9781587319150 (paperback)
LCSH: Conservatism – United States.
BISAC: SOCIAL SCIENCE / Popular Culture.
LCC JC573.2.U6 D44 2016
DDC 320.520973 – dc23 LC record available at
https://lccn.loc.gov/2016012556

∞ The paper used in this publication meets the minimum requirements of the American National Standard for Information Sciences - Permanence of Paper for Printed Materials, ANSI Z39.48-1984.

St. Augustine's Press
www.staugustine.net

I dedicate this book to my children, Francis, Adrian and Alexandra, with depthless love, and with hope that they will someday raise their own children in a nation worth conserving.

Acknowledgments

Many of these chapters began as lectures that were originally delivered at the invitation of the Intercollegiate Studies Institute, often for their wonderful summer Honors programs, for which I served as a "faculty mentor" over the course of a number of years in the 1990s and 2000s. I am especially grateful for the confidence and friendship of many fine people who worked at I.S.I. during those decades: Mark Henrie, Jeremy Beer, Jeff Cain, Jeff Nelson, Ken Cribb, Darryl Hart, Richard Brake, Mike Ratliff, Mike Andrews, Lynn Robinson, Jason Duke, Kelly Hanlon, Joel Boersma, Doug Schneider, Gary Scott, Chad Kifer, Francisco Gonzalez and Miriam Keim. Frequent companions during those summers were Peter Lawler and Daniel Mahoney who never failed to stimulate my thinking and laughter, often at the unforgettable La Boheme near Oriel College in Oxford.

I'm also grateful to Susan McWilliams, Fr. Wit Pasierbek, S.J., and Paula Olearnik of Ignatianum in Krakow, David Hessler of Montclair Kimberley Academy, Bill Campbell, former Secretary of the Philadelphia Society, and Andrew Hansen, Bryan Bademan and Matthew Kaul of MacLaurinCSF at the University of Minnesota, all of whom had the confidence in my ability to connect with students and members of the broader community.

I am grateful for a timely research grant from the Tocqueville Program for Inquiry into Religion and Public Life of the University of Notre Dame. Under the able direction of Vincent Phillip Munoz, the Tocqueville Program not only supported completion of this manuscript, but provides an extraordinary and ongoing intellectual feast for students and faculty at Notre Dame.

James Pratt of the University of Notre Dame was greatly helpful in preparing the final manuscript, and also kept up with our big puppy.

Bruce Fingerhut can't be thanked enough for his good spirits and for running a wonderful press in an era when both seem increasingly improbable. Special thanks to Peter Lawler for his interest in this collection as the first book in his new and promising St. Augustine Press series, "Dissident American Thought Today."

Lastly, my wife Inge's willingness to let me go too often made it possible for me to give these lectures. She is a blessing who daily helps me understand the meaning of grace.

Republication

Several of the chapters of this volume have been previously published in the following books and journals. The author is grateful to the Intercollegiate Studies Institute, Praeger, Rowman & Littlefield, and Heldref Publications for permission to republish these essays in this volume.

"Patriotic Vision: At Home in a World Made Strange." Intercollegiate Review, Spring, 2002.

"Ordinary Virtue." Democracy and Excellence, ed. Neil Reimer and Joseph Romance. Praeger, 2004.

"Citizenship as a Vocation." Democracy and Its Friendly Critics: Tocqueville and Political Life Today. Edited by Peter A. Lawler. Lanham, MD: Lexington Books, 2004.

"Awakening from the American Dream: The End of Escape in American Cinema? " Perspectives on Political Science 31 (Spring, 2002): 96-103.

"Manners and Morals: Or, Why You Should Not Eat the Person Sitting Next to You." Jerusalem, Athens, and Rome: Essays in Honor of Rev. James V. Schall, S.J. Ed. Marc Guerra. Augustine Press, 2013.

Contents

Introduction:
Can America Be Conserved?

Opinions about America have taken a decisively negative turn in the early part of the twenty-first century. Some 70% of Americans believe that the country is moving in the wrong direction, and half the country thinks that its best days are behind it. Most believe that their children will be less prosperous and have fewer opportunities than previous generations. Evident to all is that the political system is broken and social fabric is fraying, particularly as a growing gap between wealthy haves and left-behind have-nots increases, a hostile divide widens between faithful and secular, and deep disagreement persists over America's role in the world. Wealthy Americans continue to build gated enclaves in and around select cities where they congregate, while growing numbers of Christians compare our times to those of the late Roman empire, and ponder a fundamental withdrawal from wider American society into updated forms of Benedictine monastic communities. The signs of the times suggest that much is wrong with America.

Most analyses of our baleful situation are blinkered by two related limitations: first, our tendency to attribute our problems—and proposed solutions—almost exclusively to politics, and second, to view those solutions along an American conservative/liberal axis. Presidential elections are perceived as zero-sum games not just of governance by political coalitions, but opposing worldviews, and control of the White House specifically, and the levers of power in Washington D.C., are indicative of the pervasive role played by the federal government in managing the multifarious challenges of modern life. It matters not whether Republicans or Democrats control various institutions: to the extent that increasing and pervasive policy runs through the nation's capital, all questions of import come under its orbit and it becomes of tantamount importance that all or most of the three branches be controlled by one's preferred party.

The inescapability of Washington D.C.'s influence on every life on the planet helps explain why the partisan divide and ideological differences have deepened and intensified in recent years, rendering public institutions increasingly divided and dysfunctional. Bearing the weight of every political expectation, the battle over control and direction of our governmental institutions takes on titanic proportions, and demands a scorched-earth electoral and governing philosophy that has the pervasive effect of disgusting and disillusioning the broader electorate. As that disillusionment and disconnection deepens, committed ideologues in each party assume control of an electoral process rigged to favor the most committed, exacerbating the partisan divide and increasing civic disillusion. A vicious and seeming unbreakable cycle appears to be in full force.

Yet that divide is fundamentally illusory, as the alternations of the parties does not result in dislocating change as opposing ideologies assume control of government, but rather a consistent and ongoing continuity in the basic trajectory of modern liberal democracy, both at home and abroad. A steady increase of power to political actors in national and international capitals corresponds with concentrations of economic power among a narrowing set of global actors. These figures move continuously back and forth between public and private positions, controlling the major institutions of modern society—from schools to universities to media to government to business—blurring the line between public and private power, and building a new permanent aristocracy based upon wealth that would have made earls and dukes of old blush. The political Left—often the greatest beneficiaries of these global arrangements, and dominant players on its stage—are largely silent on their own complicity in these arrangements, and focus their energies on eradicating the inequalities of stray words and unacceptable thoughts focused on identity and especially sexual politics. The political Right promises to shore up traditional and family values while supporting a borderless and dislocating economic system that destabilizes family life especially among those who do not ascend to the global elite, those outside the elite circles who exhibit devastating levels of familial and communal disintegration.

The Right especially blames the role of expanding government for America's social and economic disarray, and calls for a return to Constitutional principles of limited government, negative rights as protections of individual liberty, and economic laissez-faire. The Left blames the rise of individualism as the source of fraying social bonds and calls for an enveloping national and even global "community" to provide both equal opportunity and equal security. For the Right, answers to contemporary problems lie primarily in liberating the Market; for the Left, solutions lie in providing government assistance. Voters are asked to take sides between these two solutions, but their misgivings about the broader political system reflect unarticulated dissatisfaction with a fundamentally false choice.

This false choice is embedded deep within American philosophic principles, and instantiated in our governing political philosophy. Enlightenment and liberal philosophies that informed the American founding posited the existence of radically autonomous human beings in the "state of nature," rights-bearing creatures who consent to the creation of a government which exists to secure those rights. This basic construct that informs the philosophy of the American Declaration of Independence and the Constitution reveals the deeper truth that is masked by our purported electoral choices: government is brought into existence to bring into *reality* the basic experience of individual autonomy that in fact exists only *in theory* in liberal philosophy. Liberal theory posits we are *by nature* "free and independent," but no human being anywhere has ever come into the world, nor been raised to maturity as "free and independent" creatures. We are rather creatures of duty, obligation and—one hopes—gratitude who are born, and most often live and die, dependent upon others. The great task of civilizations has been to sustain and support familial, social and cultural structures and practices that perpetuate and deepen personal and intergenerational forms of obligation and gratitude, of duty and indebtedness. However, liberal philosophy is based on the theoretical construct that humans are by nature autonomous, free and independent, and that it is the role and function of the State to *realize* personal, national and even globalized individualism. What liberal theory purports to be our condition according to *nature* in fact must be arranged by means of massive State intervention, expansion and constructs. It is hardly coincidental or accidental that the liberal State has become the most comprehensive and intrusive State system in the history of the globe—while purportedly establishing a limited government, in fact it establishes a limited *end* to government—the "securing," or better put, *creation*, of individual liberty—while necessarily taking on unlimited means to the realization of that "limited" end.

Thus, the insistent demand that we choose between protection of individual liberty and expansion of State activity masks that the two grow constantly and necessarily together: statism enables individualism, individualism demands statism. For all the claims about electoral transformations—for "Hope and Change" or "Making America Great Again"—two facts are naggingly apparent for those with eyes to see: America, like a ratchet-wrench that moves only in one direction, constantly becomes more individualist and more statist. This is not because one party advances individualism without cutting back on statism while the other achieves (and fails) in the opposite direction; rather, both move simultaneously together, as a matter of systemic logic that follows our deepest philosophic premises.

What is especially masked by our purported choices between primary allegiance to the Market, on the one hand, and the State, on the other, is that both "choices" advance a basic commitment to *depersonalization* and *abstraction*. Our main political choices come down to which depersonalized mechanism will purportedly secure human goods—the space of the Market which collects our billions upon billions of choices to provide for our wants and needs without demanding any specific thought or intention from us about the wants and needs of others; or the liberal State, which establishes depersonalized procedures and mechanisms for the wants and needs of others that otherwise go unmet or insufficiently addressed by the Market, via the mechanism of taxation and depersonalized distribution of goods and services. While titanic political battles are fought over which of these depersonalized and abstract forms of interaction should reign ascendant, both in fact advance simultaneously, mutually supported by each other, while together crowding out vestiges of personalized interactions that exist outside and beyond both the Market and the State. Rejected either as inefficient or selective, embedded and interpersonal structures must be displaced by the two dominant forces that increasingly rest on deracinated, global and abstracted assumptions and practices. It is revealing that two areas of greatest contemporary debate swirl around health care and education, formerly the two areas governed almost exclusively by long cultural traditions of interpersonal, embedded practices rooted in charity and self-sacrifice. Our debate today consists largely of whether these functions will be governed primarily by Market or State forces, with both sides with reason arguing that the proposed solution by the opposition is insufficient to the task.

The debate that most divides our country, then, is fundamentally over means, not ultimate aims. The parties that represent these respective positions concur on the basic aim of our political and social system, which is to preserve and extend depersonalization and abstraction. While these respective means have serious implications for the body politic, the apparent opposites are actually more fundamentally partisans of the regime—a regime that seeks to advance a particular ideal of human autonomy achieved by remaking a world thick with customs, settled practices, traditions and intergenerational debts and obligations, into one in which relationships are governed by impersonality and abstractions.

As set forth at the birth of the republic by James Madison, one of its main architects, the "first object of government" is protection of the "diversity in the faculties of men." Madison states in Federalist 10 that "from the protection of different and unequal faculties of acquiring property, the possession of different degrees and kinds of property immediately results . . . ." The *first object of government* enshrined in our Constitutional order is the protection of private differences, primarily distinctions that are manifest in different economic attainments, but further, whatever differences that are understood to arise from our "diversity of faculties." Our regime enshrines the priority of inviolable private difference lodged in our "faculties," and is thus designed to shape a polity and a society that removes all potential obstacles to the realization of those private differences. That is, not only does the regime seek to ensure preservation of private property rights (as many readers of this passage of the *Federalist* conclude), but to establish a comprehensive regime that ensures the greatest possible differentiation and development of those "diverse faculties."

Depersonalization and abstraction are essential in securing the primary imperative of the regime. Anything that might be thought to be "given" or inherited must be superseded by our mastery, above all, of transforming anything that might be "given" into a matter of choice and preference. Obstacles to the realization of fullest diversification of faculties arise from a host of limitations arising from both human relationships and nature. Human social forms must be fundamentally defined and understood as arbitrary and voluntarist, the consequence of free choices we make as abstract individuals. In the name of the fullest diversification of our faculties, all memberships are relativized and rendered as nothing more than options in a marketplace of memberships, from neighborhoods to clubs to religions, even to families. Thick social relationships formed especially within encompassing cultures are deeply suspect and must be undermined indirectly especially through the creation of national and ultimately global markets, or if resistant to this process, dismantled directly through the force of law and even police and military intervention. The shadow of those shaping institutions persists to the extent that they have been transformed into conveyors of abstraction, with settled neighborhoods replaced by interchangeable suburbs and families as the launching pads for deracinated individuals (units composed of diverse individuals that are constantly subject to being disassembled and variously reassembled by reconsiderations of those constitutive individuals). Individuals must be liberated from what comes to be viewed as the malignancy and oppressiveness of character-shaping cultures, freed into an anticulture comprised of cultureless, and therefore autonomous selves, who are at liberty to pursue and realize their own "diversity of faculties." Only when individuals are rootless, cultureless, history-less and context-less—depersonalized and abstracted—do we realize the ends prescribed by our regime. And yet we don't realize that we have been shaped in just this way because we understand our condition to be that of freedom, our lives to be the result of our accumulated choices, while the invisible architecture of the regime continues to exert its shaping force.

Nature comes to be viewed as a recalcitrant opponent of our ability to realize our diversity of faculties, requiring a massive project of overcoming its manifold limits, in the first instance by mastering the natural world in every possible respect—transportation, agriculture, where we settle, the course of rivers, unlimited extraction of resources, and so forth—and ultimately our own natures, such as mere bodily limits of longevity, our genetic code, and of course, sexual identity and reproduction. A major aim of the Constitutional order—the comprehensive regime that shapes us and our world—is the promotion of "progress in the useful Arts and sciences," the fruits of which are the mastery of natural limitations that otherwise inhibit the fullest expression of our "diversity of faculties." Whereas "diversity" might once have been understood to be manifested and perceived as the manifold and varied ways that humanity developed cultures and societies that might conform and live alongside the natural world, the aim of the American regime has been to define "diversity" at the level of the individual, requiring in turn a homogenized, standardized, uniform world that results from a legal, scientific, technological, educational and entertainment monoculture.

Ironically, modern American individuals come simultaneously to regard themselves as self-made self-makers, no longer detecting the pervasive order that shapes their identity and self-conception. The citizenry increasingly conforms to the stated aims of the Constitutional order, its first object being the protection and encouragement of the "diversity of faculties." A form of uniformity becomes the defining feature of such people: rather than a patchwork of variegated ways of life, a people shaped toward the end of diversity become increasingly identical: secure in their belief in being self-made self-makers, those identities become expressions of well-designed, market-tested identity fashions, superficially covering a self without deep content, without historical memory or cultural formation. The word "citizen" is imperceptibly replaced by the word "consumer," with even the processes of politics itself—once believed to be the domain of the common good—becoming yet another expression of consumerist preferences. The public becomes the servant of our private wants and expressions: America becomes not a *res publica*, but a *res idiotica*—in its root Greek meaning, concerned solely with private things.

What increasingly binds the polity together is a common commitment to "diversity of faculties," a widespread social norm backed by legal mechanisms to enforce devotion to indifference. Non-judgmentalism becomes the sole civic requirement, the default form of civic education, the only acceptable and increasingly enforceable norm. Civic denunciation, social ostracism, and even legal punishment is increasingly imposed upon those who profess opposition to indifference, who insist upon the ancient imperative that they are their brothers' and sisters' keepers. This social and legal opprobrium falls disproportionately upon religious believers whose basic commandment demands resistance to the societal commitment to indifference. To those who dare judge and call for action on behalf of judgment is brought down swift and fearful judgment in the name of indifference.

For many decades these trends have been evident to those rightly alarmed at the rise of those whom Tocqueville described would be trapped "in the solitude of their own hearts," the "last men" of Nietzsche's most discerning prediction. A vigorous and often successful political movement—supported extensively by committed religious believers—arose in defense of a passing age. Adopting the label "Conservative," and ascendant for some thirty years with the election of the unelectable Ronald Reagan, and thereafter a succession of proudly conservative Republican presidents (along with a triangulating Democrat), and with Congress and State governments often controlled by Republicans, for several decades it seemed that America could be conserved from baleful trends.

And yet, remarkably, the conservative ascendancy of the late twentieth and early twenty-first centuries consisted primarily in asserting the primacy of America's Constitutional—i.e., liberal—principles. Two paramount commitments were continuously articulated by politicians, opinion leaders, and academics during this period: first, strenuous defense of a relatively unregulated market as the best means of ensuring personal liberty and prosperity; and, second, insistence upon a strong military posture that extended American power into every corner of the world, often explicitly in defense of promoting universalized liberal democracy (culminating in the Wilsonian Second Inaugural address of George W. Bush). While it is also true that conservatism also attracted significant support from religious conservatives—especially evangelical Protestants and orthodox Catholics—particularly in response to the national legalization of abortion following the Supreme Court's holding in *Roe vs. Wade* in 1973, successive Republican administrations promised action on that front through the indirect appointment of Supreme Court Justices (which had the tendency of backfiring, as the examples of Anthony Kennedy and David Souter attest), whereas its military and economic commitments were pursued as matters of legislative and executive policy priorities.

"Conservatism's" two primary commitments were effectively continuous with the original aims of the liberal Constitutional project, which was advanced explicitly to undermine strong identification with traditional ways of life and cultural differentiation that might otherwise resist the nationalizing and homogenizing force of both market and militarism. American "conservatism" was fundamentally liberal in its commitments and actions, seeing its greatest threat from the communist regime of the Soviet Union, and employing the liberal tools of the American constitutional order to combat this threat, even as those very tools were undermining any remnant of a conservative way of life. At the other side of what has been a half-century project of rehabilitating conservatism in America, the current state of conservatism reveals that its ambitions were utterly unfulfilled and it has been all but routed as a governing philosophy. This outcome is not, however, because what came to be called "conservatism" failed, but because it was wildly successful.

Conservatism is inherently a reactive political philosophy, becoming visible and explicit as a political alternative due to the advances of liberal philosophy. While the first defenses of conservatism argued on behalf of traditions, practices and even prejudices—as articulated most famously by Edmund Burke—twentieth-century American conservatism invoked *liberalism* as a more "conservative" alternative to the competing ideologies of Fascism and Communism. "Conservatism" thus ended up advancing policies and promoting priorities and advancing commitments that undermined practices and traditions that might conserve distinctive

ways of life, such as farming, family-owned businesses; it failed to dis-
courage economic and cultural "globalization" toward the end of providing stability to working people; and undermined colleges as
distinctive communities and cultures of learning (i.e., the very essence
of "multiculturalism" which conservatives arrayed against in the 1980s);
and so on. Yet twentieth-century "conservatism," so-called, especially
stressed commitments to the abstractions of markets and the abstractions
of national allegiance, contributing to the evisceration of more local
forms of life and various cultural practices, with encouragement for market forces to be introduced into every aspect of life, along with calls to
devotion to the abstractions of the Declaration and the Constitution.
"Conservatism" conserved almost nothing.

We live in a thoroughgoing liberal society—the first nation founded
by the explicit embrace of liberal philosophy, and whose citizenry is
shaped almost entirely by its commitments and vision. Liberalism as a
philosophy and practice is the world's first ideology, the first political
architecture that proposes transforming all aspect of human life to conform to a preconceived political plan. However, unlike the horrific
regimes that arose in dedication to advancing the ideologies of Fascism
and Communism, liberalism is far more humane, and thus also far more
insidious: as an ideology, it pretends to neutrality, of having no preference or shaping force over the souls of humanity under its rule. It ingra-
tiates by invitation to the pleasures and attractions of freedom and
wealth. It makes itself invisible, much like an operating system on a computer goes largely unseen—until it malfunctions or crashes. Liberalism
becomes daily more visible to us precisely because its deformations are
becoming too obvious and visible to ignore. Liberals propose that what's
needed is an extension and perfection of liberalism; conservatives respond, let's expand liberalism. As Socrates tells us in Plato's *Republic*,
most humans in most times and places occupy a cave, believing it to be
simple reality. What's most insidious about the cave that we occupy is
that its walls are like the backdrop of old movie sets, promising seemingly endless vistas without constraints or limits, and thus whose walls
and method of containment are invisible to us, indiscernible as a cavern
that constrains our capacity to see and discern the nature of our confine-
ment.

The great political diagnostician, Alexis de Tocqueville, understood the nature of the cave that humanity was entering. He urged his fellow Europeans not to engage in a bootless frontal resistance to democracy's advance, but to discern its shaping power and to consciously deny, where possible, its comprehensive shaping power. Above all, he urged his readers to maintain pre-liberal and pre-democratic practices that would come under assault and duress by the insistent demands of individualism, equality and abstraction. Among these points of resistance to liberal self-immolation were local self-rule, the "arts of association," aristocratic vestiges such as law as a training in restraint, calls to self-sacrifice (e.g., chivalry), insistence upon "forms" such as the formalities of manners and liturgy, commitments to family and place, and above all, recognition and worship of God, the vertical Logos amid the horizontal democratic mass, acknowledged and thanked as matter of indebtedness and gratitude.

Tocqueville argued that what was worth conserving were ways of life and practices that liberal democracy would relentlessly seek to disassemble and, once destroyed, would never be easily replicated or re-created. The dying gasps of a "conservative" reaction to that disassembling only accelerated liberalism's self-destruction—including the demise of a "conservatism" that by its very nature could not conserve. We have reached a culminating moment when it is less a political movement that is needed—as important as it might be to seek certain public goods—than a revival of culture, of sustainable practices and defensible ways of life born of shared experience, memory and trust. However, such a revival can't occur by attempting to go back or recover something lost. Rather, ironically what is needed is provided by the very vehicle of destruction, and found amid the strengths of liberalism itself: the creative human capacity of reinvention and new beginnings. If anything is to be conserved amid a devastated landscape of a thoroughly disassembled culture, then it must be first built anew. If there is to be an America worth conserving, it must be founded again, now explicitly in departure from the philosophic principles that animated its liberal founding, appropriating those structures and even the language of liberty and rights to build anew a civilization worthy of preservation. Rather than embrace a "conservatism" that simply if creatively destroys inherited practices and ways of life, a second sailing is most needful: the re-founding of an America worth conserving.

In the essays that follow, I hope to offer a fuller diagnosis of our moment, and intimate a way forward. Correctives lie both in an adequate understanding of the past and a willingness to live adventurously and creatively into the future. A conservatism worthy of the name, if it is to come into being, must leave behind the current ruins of our liberal past and build anew a future after liberalism finally worthy of conserving.

Part 1
Hope amid the Ruins

Chapter 1
Patriotic Vision:
At Home in a World Made Strange

Patriotism exhibits an unarticulated agreement with Aristotle's great and challenging assertion that "all men are by nature political animals." According to Aristotle, humanity in full flourishing requires the goods that a political community affords the material goods of sustenance, shelter, protection by an organized defense, and the less quantifiable goods of education, the bonds of friendship, the opportunity for contemplation. Patriotism is the recognition of a debt. Individual human flourishing rests upon a sufficiently good regime, and individuality exists not "by nature" but instead requires the antecedent institutions and practices of a city. Thus, Aristotle argues, "the city is by nature prior to the household and to each one of us taken singly." To be fully human requires cultivation in a political community, a cultivation that is unnecessary for "beasts or gods" since they are incapable, or not in need, of such sustenance, but necessary for human beings, ironically, in order that they can become fully human. Patriotism, as an acknowledgment of the debts owed to particular origins and as a defense of the institutions and practices that constitute us, is an echo of this Aristotelian understanding of the relation of wholes to parts.

Yet if patriotism is a laudable expression of gratitude and perhaps even a requirement for human nobility, at the same time Aristotle reminds us that a "good citizen" is only rarely "a good man." It is a rare polity that does not call upon its citizens at times to act ignobly, at odds with virtue. Thus, if the love of one's own is a core political requirement, at the same time it remains one of the most persistent threats to justice. Patriotism, that form of loyalty that extends our souls beyond the familial and the amicable, represents one of the most potentially ennobling and potentially degrading forms of love. It at once directs our devotion to that which makes human flourishing possible, the polity, and yet ever portends the transformation of that devotion into blind obeisance, impassioned intolerance, and willing collaboration with that which is unjust and even evil.

Thought and virtue demand a limit to our love. We should not love that which is unjust, or that which inclines us to act unjustly or acquiesce in injustice. We should not love any person or place that would make us worse by dint of our love. We should love no one, and no thing, without reservation. And yet loyalty, to be meaningful, requires that we love that which is imperfect, even morally frail. The core feature of loyalty would be lost if we abandoned those people or places we otherwise cherish at the first sign of moral imperfection. Indeed, an inclination to avoid all forms of injustice would preclude the possibility of our loving in the first place. At critical moments, it is precisely our loyalty that compels us to abide with that to which we have dedicated ourselves, even given these frailties. Indeed, perhaps *because* of imperfections, our loyalty demands that we re-double efforts to support, reprimand, and improve those people, things, or places we love.

Clearly there can be no formula for navigating the calm seas and the submerged shoals of patriotism: it is neither morally defensible to demand an unreflective patriotism from a citizenry nor humanly virtuous to call for its cessation. Yet the idea of "balancing" patriotism with the critical distance demanded of universal moral claims seems ultimately to defeat the necessary priority required by patriotism. How can this tension be maintained without betraying the demands of each? If "balance" hollows out the core loyalties of patriotism, then must one simply decide one way or the other: between the love of one's own and the love of one's own virtue?

To love one's own seems to be the "default" position of most human beings. We begin our lives loving what is nearest to us, including our parents, our siblings, our childhood friends, as well as our home town, our region, our homeland. We understand the essence of growing up and the central purpose of education to be the process of moving us away from such automatic loves. Without necessarily leaving behind our first loves, we learn that our parents are not omnipotent, that our home towns are repositories of conventionality and parochialism, that our country is marred by episodes of injustice and cruelty. We move psychically and physically away from these people and places, choosing our own friends and lovers, creating our own families, exploring new towns and regions and nations. We create ever greater critical distance between our unchosen primary loves and our conscious, mature loyalties.

This movement away from unchosen commitments by means of a consideration of, and eventual dedication to, a particular choice among alternative loves is mimicked in its own way by the enterprise of political theory. As an educator in political theory myself, it is part of my vocation to challenge all those loyalties with which students enter college. Political theory often does, and by some lights always should, teach us one thing above all: a rejection of patriotism. Patriotism is one of the most impassioned "loves of one's own," a sentiment of affection for the place of one's birth and upbringing, and for the ways of life and traditions of a particular people. Political theory, on the other hand, teaches us at some level about the (mere) conventionality of every way of life. The theoretical study of politics compels us to recognize the insufficiencies of all political forms, to appreciate the virtues of regimes and traditions that are not our own. It points ultimately to the question of the best regime, a regime of perfect justice which, while implausible if not impossible, nevertheless always stands as an accusation against all existing regimes, even, and perhaps especially, one's own.

It is no accident that political theory should call patriotism into question. The word "theory" comes from the ancient Greek word *theorein*, meaning "to see." Over time, it came to describe a special and intensified form of "seeing" in the Greek world. Certain designated city officials—*theoroi*—were charged with the task of visiting other cities, to "see" events such as religious or theatrical or athletic festivals, and to return to their home city, where they would then give an account of what they had seen. To "theorize" was to take part in a sacred journey, an encounter with the "other" in which the theorist would attempt to comprehend, assess, compare, and then, in the idiom of his own city, explain what had been seen to his fellow citizens. This encounter would inevitably raise questions about the customs or practices of the theorist's own city. Why do we do things this way? Might there be a better way of organizing the regime? Might there be a *best* way of life that is not our way?

This tension between the theorist's role as critic and the city's imperative to protect its way of life is deeply embedded in the history and the practice of political theory. The full implication of that tension was revealed when Socrates was accused of impiety toward the gods of Athens and of "corrupting the youth" and was subsequently put to death after being found guilty at his trial. Throughout the Platonic corpus—which idealizes, dramatizes, and "theorizes" the life of Socrates—there is constant evidence of the abiding tension between the role of the theorist and the exigencies of the city. In his most famous dialogue, the *Republic*, we discover that Socrates has "descended" beyond the walls of the city of Athens to the multicultural port city of Piraeus, where he has gone to "see" a festival celebrating a new, foreign goddess who is being accepted into the Athenian religious world. While Socrates expresses appreciation for the Athenian procession, he expresses even greater admiration for that of the "foreigners," the Thracian worshipers. It is there, "outside" the city, in the midst of "theoretical" activity, that Socrates undertakes his most radical political enterprise—the description of the perfectly just political regime, one fundamentally at odds with the Athenian regime and all existing regimes.

By this estimation, a theorist is in some respects defined by a kind of "outsideness," an alienation originally induced by the experience of physically moving from one place to another in order to assess the virtues and vices of one's own cultural practices. Although we have largely forgotten the original meaning of the word, we still consider "theory" to involve at least the internal ability to raise questions about accepted norms and customs and to provide a critical distance that in many instances expressly confronts a nation's patriotic sensibilities.

It is thus not surprising that political theorists of many stripes have been suspicious, if not downright hostile, toward patriotism. This has been more common for thinkers on the Left—such as Emma Goldman, who wrote an essay entitled "Patriotism, A Menace to Liberty"—but it is not unknown among thinkers on the Right, such as Samuel Johnson, who more famously declared that "Patriotism is the last refuge of scoundrels." There are good reasons for thoughtful people to be suspicious of patriotism. We do not admire the evident patriotism of the German people under the Nazi regime. A story like "The Lottery" reminds us that the unquestioned acceptance of custom can support wholly malignant practices that continue in the name of "the way we do things here." An ancient play like Sophocles' *Antigone* suggests the limits of patriotism when fundamental obligations, such as religious ones, conflict with the demands of the state. People of varying ethical and religious backgrounds, from St. Augustine writing as a Christian, to Martha Nussbaum writing as a secular liberal ethicist, criticize the place of primacy that nations presume to hold under a widespread patriotic sentiment. A thoughtful person should never blindly sacrifice his "theoretical" perspective before the altar of patriotism.

Does this mean that it is impossible for a thoughtful person to be patriotic? Does this require that "theorists" should by default view the actions and claims of the state with a skeptical eye? Are "theoretical vision" and patriotism mutually exclusive?

Returning to the original practice of "theory," we can see that quite the opposite is true. The "theorist" was a designated office in the city. To "theorize" was a requirement of particular regimes in antiquity. Part of the self-definition of ancient cities involved the practice of calling their own practices into question. The activity of "seeing" foreign ways of life comprised only half of the theorist's duty. The other half, just as essential, was the "giving an account" of what the theorist had seen. This could not be done by employing the concepts and language of the foreign city, for to do so would make it nearly impossible for the theorist's fellow citizens to begin to form an understanding of exotic foreign practices. Instead, the theorist delivered his report firmly in the idiom of his own city: the position required a man deeply versed in his own language, his own customs and way of life; indeed, the office required a man deeply sympathetic to the patterns of thought and action that characterized his native city. A "theorist" would betray his office if he were, so to speak, to "go native" while abroad: no Athenian "theorist" could conceivably observe a Spartan gymnastic festival and then simply return in a condemnatory stance toward his own city. Even if a "theorist" were persuaded that foreign practices were superior to those of his own city, the primacy of the theorist's allegiance to his own city demanded the careful and prudent explanation of those practices to his fellow citizens, presented in ways that sought to evoke similar admiration by means of native assumptions and shared understandings.

Such gradualist explanations were not handed down from a position of superiority or greater knowingness by the theorist, but rather were indelibly informed by a prior respect for the practices of the theorist's own city. For even if imperfect, those practices were nevertheless the source of other civic virtues—the bases of which might be undermined if insufficiently appreciated in an indiscriminate embrace of foreign practices. Those practices were, as well, the source of prejudices that, if directly confronted, would produce a hostile reaction to the theorist's account, thereby defeating prospects for amelioration.

The theorist was chosen, then, not only for a recognized ability to "see" and apprehend with sensitivity the new and unusual, but equally for his abiding appreciation for the customs and practices of his own way of life. These are not mutually exclusive qualities, but intimately connected. A theorist was, by definition a patriot—one who treasured his cultural inheritance and traditions, knew intimately the stories and histories of his homeland, and saw these as fundamentally constitutive of his identity. At the same time, it was by means of deep familiarity and love for that cultural inheritance that the theorist was able to move fellow citizens to a renewed devotion to those practices, in some instances, or to subtle questioning of dubious customs, in others.

One sees a form of "patriotic theory" particularly in the works of the ancient playwrights. The connection between "theory" and "theater" is more than linguistic, for the ancient playwrights were a species of "theorist"—people of intense vision—who by means of their "accounts" made possible a form of "theorizing" for the city's wider citizenry as well. The playwrights retold old stories about the city and expanded on well-known tales and legends like those of Oedipus and Theseus and Orestes. By doing so, these theatrical theorists at once tapped into the constitutive material that informed their own perceptions of the foreign, while altering the ancient tales in ways that could open new vistas and ways of thinking for their audiences. The *Oresteia* or the Theban trilogy might begin in foreign cities—might, like the theoretical journey itself, take one outside the city gates, if only figuratively—but, significantly, each of those play cycles concludes in Athens. In each case the trilogy demonstrated to the Athenians their own best qualities—their system of self-governance, for instance, or their openness to foreigners (thus reaffirming the value of "theorizing" and theater)—by means of recalling and recasting ancient stories. An Athenian audience could celebrate the unique features that constituted the Athenian character, leaving the audience more consciously patriotic, and yet also newly aware of potential shortcomings embedded as warnings in the subtle but familiar retellings by Aeschylus, Sophocles, and kindred theorists.

The city, in effect, pre-committed itself to a course of potential change and improvement by means of selecting the appropriate *theoroi*. Without knowing the kinds of accounts with which it would be confronted, the city relied upon the theorist's reservoir of patriotism to ensure that the city's vital customs and practices were, in the first instance, valued and respected, and yet potentially subject to reconsideration. One might even say that the prospects for patriotism were extended and broadened by these practices. Reliance on the *theoroi* precluded the possibility of encrusted forms of parochialism or unquestioned yet vile customs, while it also undermined the accusatory claims of ungrateful cosmopolitans, "citizens of nowhere," whose initial stance was always one of hostility, mistrust, and ingratitude toward any existing city. "Theory" kept the city open to improvement without loosening the ancient loyalties. It helped to make the city a worthwhile object of devotion, in some respects anticipating Edmund Burke's observation that "To make us love our country, our country ought to be lovely."

The patriotic vision of the "theorist" eventually came to exist independently of the actual office sanctioned by the ancient city, and in particular, came to be closely associated with the form of inquiry of the ancient philosopher. In a certain respect Socrates seems to represent the pure opposite of the activity of the "theorist," since he famously did not travel outside the city of Athens except as a soldier during several battles in the Peloponnesian War. Yet the Platonic dialogues which feature Socrates constantly draw upon the ancient activity of the *theorist*. The dialogues demonstrate the manifold ways that Socrates "leaves" the city—by means of contemplation, by imagination, through encounters with foreign guests (like Protagoras and Gorgias) and foreign teachers (like Diotima), through encounters with foreign teachings (especially those of Sparta, Egypt, and Persia), and through many small "journeys" within Athens that provide a setting for greater philosophic journeys.

Generations of scholars have tried to explain the apparent contradiction that seems to lie at the core of Socrates' relationship to Athens. On the one hand is Socrates' firm insistence that he will pursue his philosophic mission as he understands it, even in spite of the prohibition of the city—as he announces in the *Apology*; on the other hand is his deep commitment and gratitude to the city that "created" him—as expressed in the *Crito*. Most modern commentators, failing to see the "theoretical" character of the Socratic enterprise, often try to downplay or dismiss one or the other aspect of Socrates, ending with a portrait of Socrates as alienated critic or Socrates as devoted citizen. Yet these are not mutually exclusive: by ancient understandings, they are mutually reinforcing.

In the *Apology*, Socrates reveals that he engages in his form of questioning at the behest of the gods, who have declared him the wisest of men and whom he seeks to disprove in his interrogation of any purportedly wise person. His mission, then, seems to be potentially at odds with the interests and traditions of the city, and Socrates insists that he will not cease his questioning even if commanded by the city. Yet he goes on to explain to his fellow citizens that he will persist in this activity *because of*, not *in spite of*, his devotion to the city that, as the Laws tell him in the *Crito*, "begat, nourished, and educated you, and gave you and all the other citizens a share in all the noble things we could . . . ." He insists in the *Apology* that he will continue to philosophize in order to rouse the "lazy thoroughbred" of Athens—a noble but insufficiently excellent regime—and that, while he will speak with anyone he happens to meet, "both foreigner and townsman," he will dwell more with his fellow citizens "inasmuch as you are closer to me in kin." His philosophic activity is undertaken on behalf of the city, born of the same gratitude and concern that prompted him to defend it bravely in the terrible Athenian defeats at Potidaea, Amphipolis, and Delium. For Socrates, there is an unbreakable connection between this civic loyalty and his critical activity. We misunderstand ancient "theorizing" if we do not recognize the entwinement of patriotism and philosophy.

At some point, the practice of theory moved from this more integrated relationship between patriotic sympathy and critical distance born of the "sacred journey" and became increasingly and almost exclusively a form of critique that started from a skeptical, untrusting, even accusatory perspective. While one can see such a development even in antiquity—Diogenes Laertius declared in the third century A.D. that he was *kosmou polites*, a "citizen of the cosmos"—the turning point that differentiated modern from ancient forms of theorizing, that placed the theorist in an adversarial position toward loyalty, can be traced to René Descartes.

It is often forgotten that Descartes's seminal work on "theorizing," the *Discourse on Method*, begins with autobiographical details of his many travels. His first step in the "thought experiment" by which he proceeds in a complete state of doubt about all inherited knowledge, all assumptions of what is true, all the most obvious facts of existence that arrive from the senses, notably occurs in a foreign country. During a winter spent in Germany, having "no cares or passions to trouble me, I remained the whole day shut up alone in a stove-heated room, where I had complete leisure to occupy myself with my own thoughts. One of the first of the considerations that occurred to me was that there is very often less perfection in works composed of several portions, and carried out by the hands of various masters, than in those on which one individual alone has worked."

Descartes describes the perfect antithesis of the approach of the ancient theorist: rather than proceeding from a sympathetic stance toward the inheritance of his own legacy, Descartes begins with radical suspicion toward all that has preceded him in act or thought, and especially all that is a result of the common endeavors of a community or a people. The fact that this Frenchman is in Germany as he begins these meditations only highlights the variance of his own investigations from those of the ancient theorists. He purposefully eschews the insights and experiences offered to him by an alien culture, and instead shuts himself literally within a room and figuratively within his own mind.

Descartes's presence in a foreign land is irrelevant to his approach, for he has concluded as a result of his previous travels that all human arrangements are wholly conventional, mere accrued custom and accretions of generations, and not a result of purposive, critical thought. Travel has taught him that there is nothing more to be learned from travel: he is now a cosmopolitan, a thinker without origin or destination, an occupant of earth who can contemplate equally well anywhere he should find himself. He is the precursor of and the model for the modern philosopher, a citizen of no-place but the realm of abstract thought, one who can presumably arrive at the same patterns of thought regardless of whatever nationality he might find himself: all locations are merely accidental and tenuous. A thinker like Descartes would appear to be content to think anywhere on earth.

At the same time, Descartes reveals that this apparent lack of preferences will result in certain preferences all the same. Descartes admits that ideally, such a philosopher is a kind of "free rider" on the wealth, security, generosity, and anonymity provided by modern nations, and especially by cosmopolitan cities that are sufficiently liberal as not to demand any loyalty in return. As Descartes relates, since his first investigations in Germany, "it is just eight years ago that this desire to remove myself from all places where any acquaintances were possible, and to retire to a country such as this [i.e., Holland], where the long-continued war has caused such order to be established that the armies which are maintained seem only to be of use in allowing the inhabitants to enjoy the fruits of peace with so much the more security; and where, in the crowded throng of a great and very active nation, which is more concerned with its own affairs than curious about those of others, without missing any of the conveniences of the most populous towns, I can live as solitary and retired as in deserts the most remote."

Descartes inaugurates modern philosophy's estrangement from the place where philosophy begins—among, and with, one's fellow citizens—and ultimately, modern philosophy's estrangement from the world. He is the very model of the proudly ungrateful anti-patriot. G. K. Chesterton once suggested that the "main problem for philosophers" was how to "contrive to be at once astonished at the world and yet at home in it." (And Chesterton proposed a novel in which an Englishman sails the South Seas in search of new islands, only to land in England without realizing it: all that was once familiar is now new. Chesterton was proposing an "accidental" theoretical journey, in effect, as a remedy to the pathology of modern philosophy.) Descartes seems not even to have acknowledged either "wonder" or "belonging" as having any intrinsic value. By making himself a stranger from his fellows and from the world, he made it impossible to be astonished by it.

Anyone who has encountered members of the "peace movement" in the aftermath of the attacks of September 11 is all too familiar with the assumptions of the Cartesian thinker and "citizen." Beneficiaries of the American regime—a political community that affords nearly countless opportunities for inquiry, life choices, and forms of expression— these critics of America tend to be among our most "cosmopolitan," and most Cartesian, in enjoying "the fruits of peace" without any gratitude or acknowledgment of their costs. Often, those who have benefited most from the great openness of our regime have been quickest to denounce the deficiencies of their country.

At the same time, undoubtedly in response to the shamelessness of these critics whose first reaction to the murder of thousands of fellow citizens was an expression of barely contained abhorrence of their own country, there have been many who in a similarly automatic way have embraced the opposite pole of unreflective patriotism. Both positions betray the complex but richly productive approach of the "theoretical patriot," rightly understood. Modernity has made this ancient position more difficult to sustain, given modernity's tendency to create dichotomies and subsequently force a choice between paradigms of freedom and those of restraint. Antiquity understood the falsity of such choices, rather acknowledging and employing the theorist's initial gratitude toward his city, and rightly viewing the theorist's role as part of the city's self-definition. The "comparative" mission of the theorist, one that brought the theorist out of the city both physically and psychically, was part of the city's own custom, and hence the theorist could never understand his activity as existing at some abstract level wholly apart from the city. The theorist, if critical of his own city, was a loving, loyal, grateful, and committed critic, not hostile or ungrateful.

After September 11, it is all the more imperative that we citizens of a democratic country make that "sacred journey" of the theorist, one that intensifies our vision, one that starts and ends in gratitude, and from which we may hope to deepen those devotions that America deserves— and that, through such patriotic vision, it will deserve ever more.

Portions of this piece were originally written for a panel presentation in which I participated at Princeton University—where I was teaching at the time—shortly after the attacks of September 11, 2001. They were eventually developed into an article commissioned by the Intercollegiate Studies Institute for a 2002 issue of Intercollegiate Review dedicated to reflections on the attacks of September 11, 2001. It was one of the first pieces that I published at the very beginning of my academic career, while an assistant professor at Princeton University. It is a topic that has informed much of my thinking to this day, particularly regarding both the requirements and limits of patriotism to any nation, and to America in particular.

Chapter 2
Citizenship as a Vocation

I. The Restless American

Tocqueville was among the first commentators on the American scene to speak of the "restlessness," or "restiveness" of democratic man.[1] Tormented by the openness of democratic society born of the universal "equality of conditions"—allowing the possibility of meteoric ascent and headlong decline—democratic man is denied a resting place, since to rest is to submit to drift, and to drift in a democratic age is tantamount to sinking.[2] In spite of the "well-being" of democratic man, he is "*inquiet*": literally, incapable of silence, therefore resistant to reflection and philosophy.[3] Democratic man seeks always to peer

---

1   Most previous translators have rendered "*inquiet*" as "restless." Harvey C. Mansfield and Delba Winthrop employ instead "restive," which in their view more fully captures Tocqueville's sense of "rebelliousness and intent," rather than the more random sense of "restless" (Alexis de Tocqueville, *Democracy in* America, trans. Harvey C. Mansfield and Delba Winthrop [Chicago: University of Chicago Press, 2000], xciii). Since I use the latter translation in this essay I will follow the Mansfield and Winthrop usage, although I continue to miss some of the lost connotations of "restless," particularly because Tocqueville describes again and again the disinclination of democratic man to come to rest. Both words, along with *inquiet*, should be kept in mind.

2   The openness of democratic society is described throughout *Democracy in America*, but see especially I.i.3, pp. 46–52. Tocqueville describes its fevered activity in *Democracy in America* I.ii.6, pp. 231–32.

3   See Tocqueville, *Democracy in America*, II.i.1 ("I think there is no country in the civilized world where they are less occupied with philosophy than

around the next corner, fearful something better lies beyond, and thus necessarily discontent with whatever decencies of the street on which he might live. Motion and dynamism is his lot—both a promise, and a curse.

Tocqueville observed that democratic man is also more likely to be a materialist—prone to accept material explanations for most phenomena, and also equally prone toward more crass forms of "materialism" because of this—and thus more fearful of death.[4] His materialism does not make him think less of death, but it promotes activity to avoid dwelling on his fear.[5] The fear of death, and the "restiveness" (and "restlessness") it provoked, was everywhere present during his journey to America.

> The inhabitant of the United States attaches himself to the goods of this world as if he were assured of not dying, and he rushes so precipitately to grasp those that pass within his reach that one would say he fears at each instant he will cease to live before he has enjoyed them. He grasps them all but without clutching them, and he soon allows them

in the United States," 403), and II.i.10 ("Why Americans Apply Themselves to the Practice of the Sciences Rather than to the Theory").

4 Tocqueville, *Democracy in America* II.i.1: "The American way of taking the rule of their judgment only from themselves leads them to other habits of mind. As they see that they manage to resolve unaided all the little difficulties that practical life presents, they easily conclude that everything in the world is explicable and nothing exceeds the bounds of intelligence. Thus they willingly deny what they cannot comprehend: that gives them little faith in the extraordinary and an almost invincible distaste for the supernatural" (404). See also II.ii.10–11.

5 The modern democratic man *par excellence* is Jack Gladney in Don DeLillo's novel *White Noise*. He and his wife Babette seek out an experimental drug that in no way extends life, but instead promises to reduce the fear of death. As Peter Augustine Lawler has pointed out, even the achievement of near-infinite life-spans would not reduce the fear of (accidental) death; it would, in fact, make such fear more keen, and spur the development of similar fear-reducing therapies.

to escape from his hands so as to run after new enjoyments.

Nor is the lifespan of any man long enough to allow for the realization of the fruitlessness of this restless condition. His fears outweigh the human desire for contentment, even to the moment of his death. "Death finally comes, and it stops him before he has grown weary of this fruitless pursuit of a complete felicity that always flees from him."[6]

Though materially more prosperous than any but the highest class in aristocratic societies, democratic man is marked by desperation born of the openness of democratic society and exacerbated by his materialism. This imperative to remain in motion makes democratic man less likely to see a project through to its fruition, to cease effort in an activity even at the very moment that project might come to fruition. This is particularly worrisome in a democracy, since it is the citizens of a democracy that are ultimately accountable for maintaining the interest and will in political projects that may require forbearance, equanimity, and patience.[7] Complexities of political life—already a spur to incline democratic man to turn away from the indignities of public life and toward the more promising if more limited possibility of accomplishment in private life—incline democratic man to be fickle in political affairs.

The inconstancy born of this anxiety is not limited to public life; indeed, it is much more obviously manifested in the frenetic activity in private affairs, where most of democratic man's endeavors occur.

6   Tocqueville, *Democracy in America*, II.ii.13, p. 512.
7   See Tocqueville, *Democracy in America* I.ii.6: "The government of one alone . . . puts more coherence into its undertakings than the multitude; it shows more perseverance, more of an idea of ensemble, more perfection of detail, a more just discernment in the choice of men . . . . Democracy . . . does not present to the eye administrative regularity and methodical order in government; that is true. Democratic government does not execute each of its undertakings with the same perfection as intelligent despotism; often it abandons them before having received their fruit, or it risks dangerous ones . . . ." (234).

> In the United States, a man carefully builds a dwelling in which to pass his declining years, and he sells it while the roof is being laid; he plants a garden and he rents it out just as he was going to taste its fruits; he clears a field and leaves to others the care of harvesting its crops. He embraces a profession and quits it.

This inconstancy in personal affairs, as well as political undertakings, reflects democratic man's pragmatic commitments, but also suggests that democratic man is less capable of achieving a comprehensive understanding of how his public and private work contribute to and sustain social and political life, and thus how one's most important activities are reflections of deeper commitments of the soul. Democratic man's public and private work are likely to be undertaken for superficial reasons, and any understanding of how one's professional and civic actions relate to activities of other citizens remains elusive.

Citizenship and workmanship suffer: capable neither of sustained engagement in complex political projects, nor inclined to remain long in a particular profession before choosing to engage in another, democratic man evinces a proclivity toward both public and private impulsiveness and inconstancy. Tocqueville raises a question worthy of further consideration: can it be that there is a relationship between this civic and professional restiveness, one whose solution resides in the development of a common set of civic and professional dispositions? Given the proclivity of democratic man to think of his activities as discrete and separate—not only viewing public and private activities as thoroughly disjunct, but even activities *within* what he believes to be wholly disparate spheres as largely disconnected from one another—Tocqueville points to the possibility, and even desirability, of a recovery of the idea of professional and even civic vocation.

II. The Idea of Vocation

"He embraces a profession and quits it." Stories from relatives and friends about sudden job changes and winding career paths attest to Tocqueville's perspicacity. Rarely does anyone speak in the antiquated language of "vocation"; instead, we tend to speak today more in terms of a "job" or, if we are inclined to speak in a more exalted tone, a "career." "Job" refers to a specific task that is subject to definitive conclusion: its etymology, while obscure, seems to relate to the idea of "pieces," and is first defined in my dictionary as "a piece," and thereafter as "an odd or occasional piece of work."[8] Life can be full of "jobs," each referring to kinds of work that may or may not be related to one another. By contrast, "career" is a term once used to describe horses at a gallop, and came eventually to mean "course of life." Many of us will have a variety of "jobs" over the course of our lives, and we will undoubtedly seek to understand the meaning of those disparate "pieces" by reference to thinking of them in terms of an overarching career.

These words tend to get jumbled together these days—witness the fact that, in first thinking about what kind of "job" one might someday want, or the kind of "career path" one might follow, many young people undergo some form of "vocational" testing in high school. Or, consider that there are various kinds of "vocational" schools aimed at preparing people for specific jobs or "careers" in particular fields, such as computer programming or automotive repairs. We tend to use the language of "vocation" when we are at the cusp of choosing our likely "career." Because of the momentousness of that choice, we undergo batteries of tests and highly trained experts to help us winnow the myriad choices that modern society presents us. For most of us, this the first limiting experience of our lives: after hearing endlessly from our parents that we can become anything that we wish to be, we are told for the first time that one has to *decide*, meaning that we must select one job at the exclusion of many other possibilities (we also undergo this trauma in sophomore year, when we have to choose a major). We consult our interests and try as best as possible to align these with our *talents*, sometimes even finding we are among those fortunate few whose interests and talents coincide. For many of us, vocational counseling is the process of finding out who we really *are*.

This form of internal consultation permeates the contemporary understanding of vocation. Take, for example, one recent "vocational"

---

8   *Webster's New International Dictionary*, Second Edition, v. 2 (Springfield, MA: G & C. Merriam Company, 1951), 1337.

self-help book entitled *Whistle While you Work: Heeding Your Life's Calling*. Its authors write: "our callings exist within us; they are inborn, a natural characteristic, like our hair color or whether we're right- or left-handed. But until we heed our calling, we're not living authentically; we're adopting someone else's model for who we should be." If less obvious to us than our hair color or the hand with which we write, the authors insist that each of us has a natural or "inborn" inclination to pursue a particular form of work, and that we must seek to live, above all, "authentically" by attempting to discern that true "calling" deep within ourselves.[9]

The authors of this book are correct on at least one score: the word "vocation" comes from the Latin word *vocare*, meaning "to call." A vocation is a *calling*. Though in English we reserve the word "vocation" for those rather daunting life choices, or alternatively for the utterly mundane forms of "vocational" or career training, one still sees how the concept of "calling" still underlies various understandings of work in other languages, such as German, in which one's "job" or "career" is called *Beruf*—*Ruf* meaning precisely a "Call." It's still the case in Germany that university professors can be "called"—they can receive a *Ruf* to accept a chair at a University—a mark of great distinction and prestige.

This example calls attention to the peculiarity of the "internalized" description of "calling" or "vocation" in such contemporary expressions as in *Whistle While You Work*, and which is largely representative of contemporary understandings of "calling." To find one's calling is to discern that uniquely true quality of oneself—to be "true" to oneself. Finding one's calling is akin to Thoreau's imperative to "follow the beat of a different drummer." One consults one's inner voice, the most profound depth of one's own soul, to discover one's calling: "trust thyself" writes Emerson in "Self-Reliance," and, simultaneously, trust no one else.[10]

---

9   Richard J. Leider and David A. Shapiro, *Whistle While you Work: Heeding Your Life's Calling* (San Francisco, CA: Berrett-Koehler Publishers, 2001), 18, 19.

10 Ralph Waldo Emerson, "Self-Reliance," in *Emerson: Essays and Poems* (New York: Library of America, 1983), 259. See his essay "Nature" for a characteristic dismissal of the relevance of all previous knowledge and belief that might exert an external influence upon an individual's judgment.

In direct contrast to these authors' sense that a calling is "inborn," properly speaking a call must come from *outside* oneself. Its origin comes not from within, but from a source external and separate from us. Of course, the origin of the term "vocation" is in this sense religious: the call comes from God, and young Catholic men are encouraged to open their senses and their hearts to the possibility that they are being "called" to life of piety and service, a life of ministry—what's called "vocational discernment." It would be a tortured usage of language indeed to ask a priest about his "job" satisfaction or "career" prospects; a "vocation" is part of a larger and more comprehensive set of human activities than are implied by the altogether self-referential usage of terms like "my job" or "my career." To refer to "*my* vocation" only partially accounts for its relational quality. If my "job" puts me into inevitable contact with other people, I am still likely to fix its point of origin in my own *interests* and my own *choice* (unless I am living inauthentically, in which case the presumption is that I am divided against myself and hence miserable); by contrast, a "vocation" requires receptivity on my part, and ultimately a choice by me to respond to a call, but I cannot altogether account for the original impetus by reference to myself alone.

The very language of "vocation" suggests a certain absence of complete control over one's life path. Consider how foreign to contemporary understandings of "vocational counseling" is the following sentence from a 1603 sermon entitled "A Treatise of the Vocations" by the English minister William Perkins. Perkins stated: "A vocation or calling is a certain kind of life ordained and imposed on man by God for the common good."[11] *This* idea of vocation—a call that comes from outside us, indeed, a call that is "imposed on man"—calls into question the simple assertion that one only lives "authentically" when one follows one's own inborn inclinations or interests. Vocation is not passive nor is it a form of resignation—we must open our senses to a voice outside ourselves and *choose* to accept the call—but neither does it permit the easy

11   William Perkins, "A Treatise on the Vocations"; cited in Paul Marshall, *A Kind of Life Imposed on Man: Vocation and Social Order from Tyndale to Locke* (Toronto: University of Toronto Press, 1996), 41.

assumption that all choices are wholly self-derived with an aim toward narrow self-fulfillment. Above all, the language of vocation implies an ordered whole that is comprehensive and benign. It *does not* imply that we can readily discern the whole—a calling remains, at a certain level, perceived through limited senses and fixed in a particular locus that falls short of comprehending the whole—but our willingness to open ourselves to a calling implies our belief that our work unfolds as part of a larger whole with a purpose, end, and meaning that likely remains only imperfectly perceptible to us. In spite of the contemporary usage of the word "vocational" to mean narrow training in a job choice, the origin of the term points to the way that one's work connected not only to other activities in one's life paths—one's "career"—but, more comprehensively, how one's work related to a larger whole outside and beyond one's own life.

Given that very few people today are likely to consider a religious vocation, it's fair to ask whether there remains anything relevant in the religious origins of the word "vocation," and whether it has any bearing on the consideration of the myriad possibilities that Tocqueville suggested that democratic citizens would "embrace" and thereafter "quit" in the course of their lives. Is "vocation" a term that must lose its relevance in a secular age and instead languish until it is translated into secular language—and hence undergoes mutation—by psychologists, therapists, and Nietzschean philosophers?

III. The Division of Labor

The language of "job" and "career" perhaps dominates our language for a good reason: in advanced industrial societies, it's almost pointless to attempt to think of more comprehensive connections that link all of our various forms of work. Indeed, we are all students of Adam Smith in this regard. We rely on the "invisible hand" to organize our activities; sustained reflection on our place in the fabric of the whole only stands to interfere in the smooth running of the "machine that would go of itself." The intricate division of labor of modern society permits ever-greater specialization, prosperity and expansion of opportunity that are the hallmarks of the American economic system. We undertake our "jobs" or "careers" with an aim to improving our lot in life, and only rarely—in spite of what we're told by commencement speakers—with a view to the good of the whole. Such a view of the "common good" is difficult to perceive from our limited perspective; we don't even have to speak of the impossibility of achieving a God-like perspective; it's difficult enough to fathom a sufficiently human perspective on human economic activities. Add to this insight the enormous complexity of modern industrial society—a Rube Goldberg illustration doesn't even begin to do it justice—and perhaps rightly we "tend to our own gardens" and hope that our tiny harvest will contribute, in some small way, to the betterment of mankind.

And, after all, that's what Adam Smith told us to do: produce in the first instance out of self-interest, and let the market take care of the whole. Hence the import of one of the most justly famous passages in the *Wealth of Nations*: "It is not from the benevolence of the butcher, the brewer, or the baker, that we expect our dinner, but from their regard to their own interest. We address ourselves, not to their humanity but to their self-love, and never talk to them of our own necessities but of their advantages."[12] No single producer considers how he is contributing the overall economic and social whole; each worker simply produces in order to make a profit for himself even while he reaps the benefits of a smoothly functioning division of labor in accumulating those many and various goods that a highly advanced economy produces.

The political theorist Hannah Arendt concluded that an economic system based on a highly specialized division of labor "is the exact opposite of cooperation."[13] The "invisible hand" of the market leads to a productive outcome that *resembles* cooperation. But Smith is quite explicit that our motivation is not, in any fundamental sense, cooperative in nature. We are rightly motivated by our individual desires to improve our condition, to accumulate wealth and to gain prominence in our

12   Adam Smith, *An Inquiry into the Nature and Causes of the Wealth of Nations*, Two Volumes (Indianapolis, IN: Liberty Press, 1981), I.ii.

13   Hannah Arendt, *The Human Condition*, Second Edition (Chicago: University of Chicago Press, 1998), 123.

society. We don't look to the good of the whole; the system takes care of that. But, what Arendt points to is that, from our limited perspective, we risk thinking that we achieve success by our own efforts alone, and that society will largely take care of itself. In thinking solely of our own advancement and accumulation, we deceive ourselves in thinking we are wholly self-sufficient and that our success has come solely through our own efforts. This accords with Tocqueville's description of the belief of modern democratic individuals, inclined to believe in their own puissance and self-sufficiency.[14]

Modern forms of work can become so separated from any conception of how that work relates to people with whom we live that it can result in a loss of the sense of common civic life—something that has been described alternatively by Robert Reich as leading to "the secession of the successful" or by the late Christopher Lasch as "the revolt of the elites."[15] One might work on behalf of stockholders scattered around the country or for an international clientele; one's workplace can just as easily be on a laptop or a cellular phone as it can be located amid an easily disassembled set of modular cubicles in an anonymous office park. Above all, because one's devotion is to the advancement of one's own career and own personal gain—one is exhorted and fully justified to think in terms of one's own "interest" instead of on behalf of humanity, in Adam Smith's inimitable words— it's really a distraction, and possibly even a betrayal of the economic system, to think beyond the immediate demands of one's own job.

Compare such depictions of the outcome of radically disparate and internally motivated job choices with William Perkins's words: again, "A vocation or calling is a certain kind of life ordained and imposed on man by God *for the common good*." Adam Smith would be the first to point out that the outcome of our work contributes to the "common good." Nevertheless, in Smith's view we are called upon to undertake such work *without conscious effort to discern or even to intend* such an

14   See note 4 above; also, II.ii.7, p. 496.
15   Robert B. Reich, "The Secession of the Successful," *New York Times Magazine*, 20 Jan. 1991: 16; Christopher Lasch, *The Revolt of the Elites and the Betrayal of Democracy* (New York: Norton, 1995).

outcome. By contrast, the idea of "vocation" in its older understanding demands of us thoughtful reflection on the manner in which our work, broadly understood, will contribute to the common good. We do so because our grounds for engaging in work, for seeing our life's meaningful activities, is viewed as being motivated on very different grounds than those suggested by Smith. In this view, thoroughgoing self-interest is insufficient and even damaging toward sustaining the fabric of social and political life. As Tocqueville pointed out, democratic man is not prone to such reflection. In the absence of such reflection, Tocqueville points to "self-interest well-understood" as a functional equivalent of such reflection, a "doctrine" that exerts a moderating influence upon more thoroughgoing forms of egoism, allowing democratic citizens to "combine their own well-being with that of their fellow citizens."[16] The doctrine of "self-interest well-understood," Tocqueville averred, allowed Americans in particular to justify all their actions in terms of self interest, even those that entailed a more generally beneficent (and even immediately personally disadvantageous) outcome, such as their willingness "to sacrifice a part of their time and their wealth to the good of the state." Yet, Tocqueville surmised that, over time, the language of self interest would exert a formative influence upon democratic man's self-understanding: "for one sometimes sees citizens in the United States as elsewhere abandoning themselves to the disinterested and unreflective sparks that are natural to man; but the Americans scarcely avow that they yield to movements of this kind; they would rather do honor to their philosophy than to themselves."[17]

By contrast, in aristocratic societies, the "few powerful and wealthy individuals" entertained the "sublime idea of the duties of man."[18] Tocqueville was not here sentimentalizing aristocratic noblesse oblige — after all, he doubted that men in aristocratic ages were in fact more virtuous, in spite of the greater frequency about which virtue was spoken—but without such language and concomitant encouragement, the notion of duty was likely to give way to ever more shameless actions

16 Tocqueville, *Democracy in America*, II.ii.8, p. 501.
17 Tocqueville, *Democracy in America*, II.ii.8, p. 502.
18 Tocqueville, *Democracy in America*, II.ii.8, 500.

undertaken solely out of interest and toward the end of self-aggran-dizement, and the very language of duty and sacrifice was likely to be lost, and with it the extinguishing of "disinterested and unreflective sparks that are natural to man." As language itself became coarsened under the onslaught of modern doctrines of self-interest, actions formerly praiseworthy for their selflessness would cease to be expli-cable and therefore become less recognizable: "as the imagination takes less lofty flight and each man concentrates on himself, moralists become frightened at this idea of sacrifice and they no longer dare to offer it to the human mind . . . ."[19] The possibility of aristocratic hypocrisy could serve democratic society, Tocqueville seemed to be suggesting: given the force of public opinion in democracy, the sus-taining influence of aristocratic virtue, now in democratic parlance, could both encourage and make recognizable acts undertaken out of duty and sacrifice, thereby moderating the "doctrine of self-interest," even if "well-understood."

The language of virtue came easier in aristocratic societies: one's place in the order of things was virtually unchanging and easily recog-nized, and therefore one could easily discern how one's exertions con-tributed to the greater good. For modern democratic man, the openness of the economy and society as a whole and the absence of all fixed orders makes it difficult, even impossible, to perceive one's place in the whole. In particular, the modern innovation of the "division of labor" seems to militate against any easy, or even desirable, means of perceiving how one's work contributes to the greater good. Both as workers and as citi-zens, democratic man can only perceive how his efforts advance the common good as through a glass darkly.

Tocqueville points to an older teaching in which the "division of labor" is not a justification for "minding one's own business," but in fact points us to the riddle of the human whole of which we are so many parts. As is so often the case, Tocqueville's teaching—intended as a "new political science . . . for a world altogether new"—points back to the pre-modern teachings.[20] For, there is nothing inherent to the concept of "di-

19 Tocqueville, *Democracy in America*, II.ii.8, 501.
20 Tocqueville, *Democracy in America*, "Introduction," 7.

vision of labor" that demands a neglect of considerations of how our work might contribute to the common good. Indeed, the first description of the division of labor in the Western tradition arguably points *not* to a conception of work that stresses above all *self-interest*, but rather a common acknowledgement of *mutual reliance*. This possibility is suggestively limned in the political masterwork of antiquity, the *Republic* of Plato.

While the most obvious lesson of Plato's *Republic* appears to involve either the recommendation, or perhaps the implausibility, of the rule of philosopher-kings, even those who disagree about the intended lesson regarding the philosopher king nevertheless agree that, more broadly, Plato endorses a radical division of labor in which, according to Socrates, justice consists of "the minding of one's own business."[21] Yet, this definition of justice follows upon an earlier and provisional definition that is overlooked in most treatments of the *Republic*, and which points to a radically different understanding of justice and near-opposite implications of the division of labor both from this apparent later definition within the *Republic*, and certainly from Adam Smith's understanding.

Often neglected is the very first definition of justice that precedes the development of the "feverish" city in speech (372e). This first definition occurs at the conclusion of a regrettably brief initial description of the "first" city that occurs between Socrates and Adeimantus in Book II. This first city, described by Socrates as "the city of utmost necessity" (369d), is marked by a very rudimentary division of labor. Socrates begins with the observation that "a city, as I believe, comes into existence because each of us isn't self-sufficient but is in need of much" (369b). However, nature or providence has fortunately assured that we are equal in our need and fortunately diverse: "each of us is naturally not quite like anyone else, but rather differs in his nature; [and] different men are apt for the accomplishment of different work" (370a). For this reason, Socrates suggests, it would be *selfish* for those of us with specific talents *not* to undertake that profession in a relatively exclusive fashion. Socrates says, "Must each of [these men] put

21   Plato, *Republic*, trans. Allan Bloom (New York: Basic Books, 1968), 433a.

his work at the disposition of all in common—for example, must the farmer, one man, provide food for four and spend four times as much time and labor in the provision of food and give it in common to the others; or must he *neglect* them and produce a fourth part of the food in a fourth of the time and use the other three parts for the provision of a house, clothing, and shoes, not taking the trouble to share in common with others, but *minding his own business for* himself?" (369e–370a; emphasis mine).

While Socrates describes an economic system that rests as thoroughly on a "division of labor" as that recommended by Adam Smith, the *motivations* for our engagement in work is fundamentally different: whereas in Smith we should only consult our *interests*, in Plato we engage in our particular form of work out of a kind of *generosity* to those with whom we live. We are to engage in that work for which we have special talent explicitly to avoid *neglect* of our fellow citizens, and out of a *rejection* of the idea that justice consists most fundamentally in "minding one's own business." We do so because no one of us is capable of providing the entirety of our sustenance—"because each one of us isn't self-sufficient but in need of much" (369b)—and beyond that, because no one of us is capable of creating the good things of life by ourselves alone. Thus, the too brief conversation with Adeimantus concludes with Socrates asking where one can locate justice in such a city. Adeimantus responds, haltingly, that it must rest in a recognition of our common "need" (372a).[22] Among the few non-subsistence activities in which citizens engage is worship: "After [their work] they will drink wine and, crowned with wreaths, sing of the gods. So they will have sweet intercourse with each other, and not producing children beyond their means, keeping an eye out for poverty or war" (372b). Such worship

---

22 "Need" is a translation of *chreia*, which, in addition to its meaning as lack or insufficiency, also contains connotations of "familiarity" or "intimacy." The exchange between Adeimantus and Socrates is permeated by the invocation of various words for "need," including the very outset of the decision to create a "city in speech": "Let's make a city in speech from the beginning. Our need [*chreia*], as it seems, will make it" (369c). Even political philosophy begins with an acknowledgement of its insufficiency.

reflects ultimate acknowledgment that "each of us isn't self-sufficient but is in need of much" (369b).

Smith's conception of the "division of labor," emphasizing above all our self-interest, is made possible by a background assumption imported from liberal political theory and the social contract tradition that human beings are by nature "independent and free" in John Locke's words, and that we enter society only on the basis of an appeal to calculated self-interest. Self-interest is the natural, "default" mode of human life: any appeal to "benevolence" toward humanity or generosity to one's fellow citizens is unnatural. Plato offers us an alternative conception—not one that begins with a portrait of human self-sufficiency, but rather with human *insufficiency*, one that stresses the human inability to supply our needs and wants through our own efforts alone. Even if we conclude this rudimentary city to be "a city of pigs"—as it's accused of being by Adeimantus's brother, Glaucon—we should not forget that more sophisticated and intricate societies, even the "feverish city" whose citizens come to believe that justice lies in "minding one's own business," still rest on this first acknowledgment of human *insufficiency* rather than self-sufficiency.[23]

In our own society, we are far more likely to encounter people in sympathy with an Emersonian idea of "self-reliance" rather than the

---

23 The relationship between the "two cities" is worthy of further exploration, but implicitly it certainly underlies the discussion between Socrates and Glaucon on why the philosopher-king, once having escaped and ascended above the cavern of opinion, would choose to re-descend where near-certain death awaited him. Socrates asserts "that it's not the concern of law that any one class in the city fare exceptionally well, but it contrives to bring this about for the whole city, harmonizing the citizens by persuasion and compulsion, making them share with one another the benefit that each class is able to bring to the commonwealth. And it produces such men in the city not in order that it may use them in binding one's city together, but in order that it may use them in binding the city together" (519e–520a). What once came as a natural and necessary course in the "city of utmost necessity" must now be forged by law, persuasion and compulsion in the "feverish city" in which the connections between the work of citizens, and their mutual reliance, is no longer as easily perceived.

Platonic conception of justice grounded in a recognition of need. While Adam Smith's conception of the division of labor, of course, recognizes that our own work is only part of the fabric of a larger whole, nevertheless his conception does not call for this recognition *from us*, and allows us the belief, and even the fiction, that we can be "self-reliant."

IV. Politics as a Vocation

One of the dangers of the Smithian conception of the "division of labor" is that there is the all-too-easy inclination to apply its justification, and further, to take for granted its motivations, in the public realm as well as in the private—to see the "division of labor" born of self-interested pursuit of individual good as *political* as well as *economic*.

A classic expression of the need for a division of labor in political affairs came from Benjamin Constant in his 1819 address, "The Liberty of the Ancients Compared to that of the Moderns."[24] In that speech, Constant rejected the ancient notion of liberty that rested on a belief that every citizen should participate directly in the creation of legislation since, in Constant's view, this resulted in "the complete subjection of the individual to the authority of the community. You find among them almost none of the enjoyments which . . . form part of the liberty of the moderns."[25] This notion of "positive liberty," as it was called by Isaiah Berlin, held that we are only free when we rule ourselves. Instead, Constant endorsed the modern notion of liberty—alternatively called "negative liberty"—that each individual should be free to pursue his own interest without being forced to assume the duties of civic office: "In the kind of liberty of which we are capable, the more the exercise of political rights leaves us time for our private interests, the more precious will liberty be to us. Hence, Sirs, the need

24 Benjamin Constant, "The Liberty of the Ancients Compared with that of the Moderns: Speech Given at the Athénée Royal," in *Constant: Political Writings*, ed. Biancamaria Fontana (New York: Cambridge University Press, 1988): 307–28.
25 Constant, 311.

for the representative system. The representative system is nothing but an organization by means of which a nation charges a few individuals to do what it cannot or does not wish to do herself. Poor men look after their own business; rich men hire stewards."[26] Thus, representation was recommended as a modern innovation that liberated citizens from the onerous duties of self-government, allowing individuals to direct their energies to private pursuits, above all to those economic pursuits that promoted "commerce" which in turn inspired "a vivid love of individual independence."[27] Thus, from a division of public and private labor, a more extensive division of labor within the economy is also rendered possible: time and abilities were to be freed from the constraints of political rule, permitting the concentration of activity in commercial affairs. In the view of proponents of representation such as Constant, some people would be more inclined, and more qualified, to run the public affairs of the country than others; those with dispositions and talents that ran toward public service should work on our behalf, just as those more inclined to engage in commerce would contribute to the expansion of the economy.

This explanation seems all the more attractive in the face of the modern complexity of political affairs. Faced with seemingly intractable problems of enormous nation-states (indeed, as "Publius" explains in *Federalist* 10, representation is to be combined with a large "orbit" as one means of forestalling majoritarian tyranny, with the concomitant and beneficial effect of creating a more complex polity), there is an almost unavoidable temptation to throw up one's arms in despair and rely on the expertise of others. A brief statement by President Kennedy from 1962 captures the underlying grounds for this despair:

> Most of us are conditioned for many years to have a political viewpoint—Republican or Democratic, liberal, conservative, or moderate. The fact of the matter is that most of the prob-

26 Constant, 325–26.
27 Constant, 315. See also John Stuart Mill, "Thoughts on Representative Government," ch. 3, who also links the practice of representation with the rise of "greater prosperity."

lems . . . that we now face are technical problems, are administrative problems. They are very sophisticated judgments, which do not lend themselves to the great sort of passionate movements which have stirred the country so often in the past. [They] deal with questions which are now beyond the comprehension of most men. . . .[28]

In such a way, the idea underlying the "division of labor" is extended to all spheres of life. Some people are uniquely competent to understand and direct public affairs, and others possess a greater ability in commercial affairs. A bright line is drawn between the two, with all individuals commended to concentrate upon their respective jobs.

But one can perceive at least one immediate danger in the supposition that governance ought to be left in the hands of competent political experts for whom public service is their particular *job*: on what grounds do political leaders engage in their "work"? If the grounds for the pursuit of every person's work is *self-interest*—the idea of "getting ahead"—how can it be assumed or even defended that "public servants" should keep the common good in view? How can a political structure that rests upon the suppositions of the economic structure—one which mimics the idea of "division of labor" in which each worker pursues his self-interest without any appeal to benevolence or sacrifice or duty—how can it be expected that "workers" will engage in public affairs for any reason other than personal advantage? Wouldn't the public have to regard the motives of politicians with a high degree of cynicism; and wouldn't any cases of self-enrichment simply confirm those widespread public suspicions? From where would the resources for "public service" on behalf of "common good" come in a society dominated by assumptions that all work is undertaken on the grounds of self-interest?

28 Cited in Christopher Lasch, *The Culture of Narcissism: American Life in an Age of Diminishing Expectations*, Revised Edition (New York: Norton, 1991), 77. For a classic statement of the inability of people to engage in self-government and the necessity of rule by elites, see Walter Lippmann, *Public Opinion* (New York: Touchstone, 1997).

Tocqueville recognized that public service undertaken under the prevailing imperative of self-interest was absurd—tantamount to the demise of democracy—and observed that, thankfully, the very activity required in public office counteracted such narrowness.[29] The people's representatives "cannot meddle in public affairs without having the scope of their ideas extended and without having their minds be seen to go outside their ordinary routine."[30] The constant importuning, attempts at persuasion, even deception serve to contribute to his enlightenment. "In politics, he participates in undertakings he has not conceived, but that give him a general taste for undertakings."[31]

We tend to think about democracy as a system of government that ensures maximum freedom, maximum *choice*. It is a form of government that seems to comport with the idea that we choose such things as our jobs, our careers—as well as nearly every other aspect of our lives—by reference to our *interests* and *preferences*. Yet, the example of representation focuses the mind: in light of such considerations, democracy can be seen more properly and fundamentally to rest on a set of assumptions that closely approximate the underlying basis of the *Republic*'s "first city." Democracy, by this measure, is better conceived as a political system born of an acknowledgment that no one is capable of superior rule; that no one has the final competency to determine the best course of action under every circumstance; and thus, it calls into question the very rationale of representation, if not its practice. Such considerations lead necessarily to profound doubt over a supposition such as that of Constant that "the representative system is nothing but an organization by means of which a nation charges a few individuals to do what it cannot [do] . . . ."[32] Citizenship

---

29 An important additional factor not discussed here, in addition to the very activity involved in holding office, stresses the importance of the persistence of another aristocratic virtue—honor—in democratic times. For an exploration of the requirements of honor in liberal democracy, see Sharon Krause, *Liberalism With Honor* (Cambridge, MA: Harvard University Press, 2002).

30 Tocqueville, *Democracy in America* I.ii.6, p. 233.

31 Tocqueville, *Democracy in America* I.ii.6, p. 233.

32 Constant, 325–26.

is a *calling*—it's the vocation of every person who would live in a democracy. To alter slightly the words of William Perkins: "Citizenship is a vocation or calling ordained and imposed on man for the common good *because none of us is God*"—because no one of us is born to rule, born to be a philosopher-king or even born to be a representative. We are born citizens in a certain sense—citizens, meaning "people who belong in a city or *polis*"—because, as Socrates acknowledges, we are all born in need: "each of us isn't self-sufficient but is in need [*chreia*] of much" (369b). The roots of a just city, as Plato observed millennia ago, is in the mutual recognition of our insufficiency.

V. Citizenship as a Vocation

Tocqueville recognized that modern democratic citizens would find it difficult to perceive the ways in which their private undertakings related to public life, and only dimly perceive how their individual and apparently discrete activities combined with the efforts of other citizens. Like Plato—who acknowledged that such recognition in more populated and variegated cities would require law, compulsion, and persuasion (519e–520a)—Tocqueville acknowledged that the complex nations of modern democracy would require concerted effort and the development of "art" in place of what was more readily perceived as being natural in less complex settings. "Only with difficulty does one draw a man out of himself to interest him in the destiny of the whole state, because he understands poorly the influence that the destiny of the state can exert on his lot."[33] Tocqueville insisted on the importance of engaging democratic man in local activities in which connections and implications of public work could be more readily perceived. "But should it be necessary to pass a road through his property, he will see at first glance that he has come across a relation between this small public affair and his greatest private affairs, and he will discover, without anyone's showing it to him, the tight bond that here unites a particular interest to the general interest."[34] By means of what are ofttimes involuntary immersion in immediate public

33 Tocqueville, *Democracy in America* II.ii.4, p. 487.
34 Tocqueville, *Democracy in America* II.ii.4, p. 487.

affairs, formerly narrow-minded democratic citizens begin to perceive the broader cross-currents of interests, even creating conditions in which the "heart is enlarged."[35] "When citizens are forced to be occupied with public affairs, they are necessarily drawn from the midst of their individual interests, and from time to time, torn away from the sight of themselves."[36]

Modern democracy disposes citizens to retreat from public life and pursue an endless succession of apparently unrelated "jobs" born of a disposition toward "restiveness" and restlessness. Tocqueville reminds us that democracy rests more fundamentally upon the cultivated art of perceiving the manifold ways in which our apparently discrete activities are connected to the overarching work of public life. This recognition is hard-won in democratic ages; men would rather embrace flattering portraits of their self-sufficiency and self-reliance. Democratic man comes only grudgingly to the recognition of his insufficiency and to the nobility of "aristocratic" virtues of duty and sacrifice. "One is occupied with the general interest at first by necessity and then by choice; what was calculation becomes instinct; and by dint of working for the good of one's fellow citizens, one finally picks up the habit and taste of serving them."[37] By doing more honor to ourselves than to our philosophy, we are enabled to discover the true definition of freedom, now not as a slave to narrow interest manifested as inconstancy in our work, but as liberation by a love freely given.

This chapter was based on a lecture that I delivered annually for several years in the early 2000s on the occasion of the Intercollegiate Studies Institute annual Honors Program conference in Indianapolis, IN. The conference had been originally oriented toward offering career and professional advice, and this lecture was an effort to widen out that original purpose to point to the our work as citizens and cast that responsibility in the language of vocation. The lecture was eventually revised for publication in an edited volume entitled Democracy's Friendly

---

35 Tocqueville, *Democracy in America* II.ii.5, p. 491.
36 Tocqueville, *Democracy in America* II.ii.4, p. 486.
37 Tocqueville, *Democracy in America* II.ii.4, p. 488.

Critics, edited by Peter A. Lawler. I would like to thank I.S.I. for the opportunity to reflect on these themes before a bright group of students, and in particular several staff during those years—Jeffrey Cain, Mark Henrie, and Jason Duke—for the invitation to speak before a fine group of students. Some of the informality of this essay reflects its origin as an undergraduate lecture.

Chapter 3
Ordinary Virtue

The Uncommon Commonness of Ordinary Virtue

Democracy is the government of ordinary citizens. Rarely has such a mundane statement been so trivially true. For, hidden in the adjective "ordinary" is the assumption of widespread extraordinariness. As George Santayana argued, democracy requires seemingly "ordinary" virtues that are in fact rare and exceptional:

> If a noble and civilized democracy is to subsist, the common citizen must be something of a saint and something of a hero. We see, therefore, how justly flattering and profound, and at the same time how ominous, was Montesquieu's saying that the principle of democracy is virtue.[1]

Santayana thus points out that in democracy "extraordinary" virtues—those of the "saint" and "hero"—must be "common" among the entire citizenry. The "ordinariness" of democratic virtues are all the more "extraordinary" for the presumption of their universality. Saints and heroes are notable for their rarity and exceptionalness; their virtues, deemed praiseworthy in part due to their very infrequency, must pervade the citizenry, making them at once unexceptional for their very commonness, and yet still extraordinary for their exceeding difficulty. The exceptional

---

1   George Santayana, *The Life of Reason, or The Phases of Human Progress*. One-volume edition (London: Constable & Co., Ltd, 1954), 148 (ch. 5, Reason in Society).

must become common even as the commons become exceptional. For this reason, Santayana sees democracy as the most "flattering" of political regimes because it pictures humanity at its optimistic best, while also the most "ominous" for the same reason—particularly given that Santayana was not prone to optimism.[2]

Santayana points to how such "ordinary virtues" are in most instances mundane and homely, but at base rest on a rare and profound willingness to forego external honor on behalf of what is right and even righteous; he further suggests how such "ordinary virtues" are all the more extraordinary for their generality in a civilized democracy. The "ordinary virtues" of a democracy, then, reflect the most demanding kind of virtue ever conceived: ones that are accorded little praise and often overlooked and unrecognized; ones that are only apparently easy to practice but in fact supremely difficult to manifest; ones that may call upon acts of extraordinary sacrifice, but more often are marked by quiet constancy and unobservable nobility; ones that, if not unnatural, are nevertheless not the automatic inheritance of humanity, but require cultivation in a regime that tends to be averse to compromising the freedom of individuals, hence mistrustful of such cultivation.

Thus, the "ordinary virtues" of democratic citizenship are in fact extraordinary—difficult to perceive, much less practice, and more often

---

2   Preceding his words about democratic excellence, Santayana wrote: "For such excellence to grow general mankind must be notably transformed." He was not at all sanguine at such prospects, however, as the whole of Ch. 5 ("Democracy") demonstrates. Indeed, regarding the prospect of widespread democratic virtue he states: "What might happen if the human race were immensely improved and exalted there is as yet no saying; but experience has given no example of efficacious devotion to communal ideals except in small cities, held together by close military and religious bonds and having no important relations to anything external" (147). Herbert Croly concludes *The Promise of American Life* by citing Santayana's suggestion that democracy would require the transformation of mankind, but—characteristically—takes this as a practicable recommendation and altogether ignores the pessimistic frame in which Santayana makes the observation. Herbert Croly, *The Promise of American Life* (Cambridge, MA: Harvard University Press, 1965 [1909]), 454.

than not likely to be ignored or even condemned than praised. The paradoxical and demanding nature—the necessary ordinariness of extraordinary virtue, and extraordinary nature of "ordinary virtue"—can be perceived curiously, even surprisingly, in the words and actions of the most honored of Americans, the founding generation of the American republic, and in particular among the men who affixed their names to the founding document, the Declaration of Independence. More important, finally, is the demand that we perceive such acts of nobility, and accord such acts honor, for *the right reason*. Just how extraordinary were their actions, and correspondingly, are the demands upon us, ordinary citizens, to rightly comprehend the nature of virtue (and thus in an essential sense to participate in, even exhibit such extraordinary virtue), I seek to delineate below.

Celebrating the Extraordinary

It is always startling to read John Adams's uncannily accurate prediction of the way in which Independence Day would be celebrated by future generations—but for the fact that he was off by two days:

> The second day of July 1776 will be the most memorable epoch in the history of America. I am apt to believe that it will be celebrated by succeeding generations as the great anniversary festival. It ought to be commemorated as the Day of Deliverance by solemn acts of devotion to God Almighty. It ought to be solemnized with pomp and parade, with shows, games, sports, guns, bells, bonfires, and illuminations from one end of the continent to the other from this time forward forevermore.[3]

Recent treatments of the founding generation have rightly reminded the current generation of their enormous sacrifice on behalf of an undertaking that must have seemed at times desperate and at others simply

---

3   Letter to Abigail Adams; cited in David McCullough, *John Adams* (Simon & Schuster, 2001), 130.

foolish. McCullough, for instance, in his fine biography of John Adams, stresses the difficulty with which the unlikely coalition of Adams, Jefferson and Franklin worked tirelessly to move the Continental Congress to adopt a resolution to declare independence from Great Britain. This was not an easy decision, nor necessarily the most obvious one, nor even one that was as wildly popular as we might imagine today. Though it was well-received in many places, and especially strongly supported in colonies that had had fatal encounters with the Royal armies—especially Massachusetts—it was not a "political slam-dunk." Several colonies voted against the resolution in July — including Pennsylvania, a "must-have" State at the time—and only by intense political lobbying overnight between July first and second were various royalists persuaded either to change their vote or to abstain on the following day.[4] Just as much foreboding accompanied the announcement as did celebration. After all, what the colonies had done was, in the eyes of Great Britain, commit an act of treason. A huge invading force was poised to attack the colonies, and America knew that it had almost no significant military supplies, a poorly trained number of troops that barely deserved the name "army," and no significant allies in the international arena.

When one thinks back on those men who moved the nation to declare independence, cool reflection forces one to think not of how much they stood to *gain* by gaining independence from England—for it's not obvious that many, if any, stood to gain much at all—but how much they stood to *lose* by committing this act of treason in the eyes of England. How much was at risk is highlighted not by the most famous lines in the Declaration in its second paragraph—"We hold these truths to be self-evident, that all men are created equal, that they are endowed by their Creator with certain unalienable Rights, that among these are life, liberty, and the pursuit of happiness"—but, rather, the closing words in the document. This sentence, not originally in Jefferson's draft but added by Congress during final revisions on July 4th, echoes the opening words of the Declaration—"A UNANIMOUS Declaration"—by concluding with a statement of solidarity and mutual trust: "And for the support of this Declaration, with a firm reliance upon the protection of divine

4   McCullough, *John Adams*, 125–29.

Providence, we mutually pledge to each other our Lives, our Fortunes, and our sacred Honor."

These were men with a great deal to lose—including, for most, significant fortunes by the standards of those days. In fact, as a result of signing the Declaration several of the signers were targeted by the British during the Revolution and ended their lives, in some cases, quite a bit poorer and even penniless. Close to where I once lived, in Hopewell, New Jersey, there is a grave marker in the town cemetery for John Hart, who was forced to abandon the bedside of his dying wife and live in caves for much of the duration of the war, and returned finally to find his wife had died and his children had scattered to the winds. He died shortly thereafter, alone and destitute.

What is all the more remarkable was their willingness to pledge their lives—which several did lose in the course of the revolution. The signers were keenly aware of the likelihood of execution for signing the Declaration. It's often said that Benjamin Franklin quipped, "Gentlemen, we must all hang together, or most assuredly we shall hang separately."[5] McCullough relates that when Adams, Franklin, and Rutledge met with the British General Howe after the British defeated Washington in New York City, Howe offered amnesty to some of the signers if they would rescind the Declaration. The pardons were not blanket however, and among those not listed was Adams himself.[6]

The willingness to pledge their lives for the sake of independence is remarkable especially because the first part of the document is based extensively on the political philosophy of John Locke.[7] Locke, famously, argued that political community was the result of a social contract that people formed in the State of Nature. Because the State of Nature is eventually so disadvantageous to individuals—perhaps not as awful as

---

5   Cited by McCullough, *John Adams*, 138.

6   McCullough, *John Adams*, 158.

7   Michael Zuckert has recently made a strong case for the once-popular, now contested view that the Declaration was of Lockean origin. See Michael P. Zuckert, *The Natural Rights Republic: Studies in the Foundation of the American Political Tradition* (Notre Dame, IN: University of Notre Dame Press), 1997.

Hobbes' conception of the state of nature, who described it as "nasty, brutish, and short," but not a condition that ultimately accords human beings with sufficient guarantees of security, much less justice—natural men sacrifice some of their natural freedoms to form a government that will act as an impartial judge and protector of the contracting agents. The government is charged with preserving the rights of citizens— among them "life, liberty, and property" in Locke's version—and when government encroaches too much on these rights, then we reserve the right to revolt against that government, revert back to a State of Nature and form a new social contract.

What one has to notice is that there is a tension in the basic fabric of this theory. Social Contract theory is based on the premise that we value, above all, *self-preservation*—even more than we value our total liberty, since we give up some liberties from the State of Nature in order to institute a government that can protect our lives from the depredations of others. Hobbes, for one, so feared reversion back into the State of Nature that he concluded that government could demand ANYTHING of its citizens *except* to force anyone to be *willing* to die. Even those, such as criminals, who are justly condemned to death by the State neverthe- less, according to Hobbes, maintained the right to seek to preserve them- selves to the very end. Even Locke notes that soldiers cannot be forced to fight for a State during a war, but that the superior officers have every right to shoot their own soldiers should they refuse to fight, thus forcing a calculus of which was the worst prospect—certain death at the hands of one's own officers, or possible survival against the enemy. Locke is a bit more ambiguous about what conditions would justify outright revo- lution, but the conditions have to be much worse than the worst condi- tions of the State of Nature. The government would have to be seen as more dangerous to one's own life than the perilous condition in the State of Nature. And yet, for the men who signed the Declaration, this was clearly not the case—their lives were not personally in danger before they declared independence, and their lives suddenly were in grave peril afterwards.

Liberal theory has always had a bit of a hard time dealing with this conundrum, that is, how to call on the willingness to sacrifice even one's life for the sake of the core principles of liberty, since liberalism itself places a very high premium on self-preservation. Under such a set of philosophical presuppositions, how can one be encouraged to value liberty even more than self-preservation? Tocqueville noticed this difficulty during his visit to the United States in the 1830s, remarking that democratic citizens had a tendency to justify every act in terms of self-interest, even those acts that might be justifiably construed as inspired out of generosity, sacrifice and duty, even the willingness "to sacrifice a part of their time and their wealth to the good of the state." Tocqueville surmised that, over time, the language of self-interest would exert a formative influence upon democratic man's self-understanding: "for one sometimes sees citizens in the United States as elsewhere abandoning themselves to the disinterested and unreflective sparks that are natural to man; but the Americans scarcely avow that they yield to movements of this kind; they would rather do honor to their philosophy than to themselves."[8]

John Adams in some ways—if only unconsciously—articulated the contradiction during his defense of Captain Preston, who was on trial as the commander of the British soldiers who were responsible for killing five civilians in the "Boston Massacre." He defended them—which was an unpopular thing for him to do as a rising lawyer—on the only grounds that he could, that they had fired their muskets in self-defense. In his stirring peroration he stated, "Ladies and Gentlemen, it is for this principle of Self-preservation that I would give my right arm, nay, I would give my very life . . . ."[9] It is nothing if not a delicious paradox that the "principle of self-preservation" should need to be defended by offering to give one's own life.

Classic liberal theory of Hobbes and Locke has relied, often implicitly, on the more ancient virtue of honor as a support for the protection of liberty and as a resource for promoting even the willingness to "die for the principle of Self-preservation."[10] Honor is an ancient virtue of

---

8   *Democracy in America*, trans. Harvey C. Mansfield and Delba Winthrop (Chicago: University of Chicago Press, 2000), II.ii.8, p. 502.

9   Cited by Wilson Carey McWilliams in "The Alternative Tradition"; available at http://www.libertynet.org/~edcivic/civical.html.

10 Tocqueville recognized that democracies would require the persistence of such aristocratic virtues such as honor in order to resist the tendency toward

aristocratic, often warrior societies, portrayed perhaps most famously in ancient epics like the *Iliad* and the *Odyssey*. Honor is bestowed on those of great virtue, especially military virtues like courage in the Homeric epics. Indeed, the basic story of the *Iliad* is about what happens when a hero of great courage is dishonored by being withheld the material marks of recognition and honor that served as recompense for the willingness to die without the prospect of a beneficent afterlife.[11] Agamemnon withholds from Achilles some "spoils" of war—a captive woman—and Achilles withdraws from the battlefield. It's not a matter of material loss—Achilles is a wealthy king, and already possesses many such "spoils." When Agamemnon tries to make good, he offers much more wealth and many more captive women than he originally withheld, but at this point none of this can appease Achilles. To be willing to die and have one's eternal soul thrown into the horrible pits of Hades, one must at least know that one will be honored after one's life has ended. With his honor suddenly withdrawn, Achilles begins to value his life for what it is, even now preferring a long ordinary life to the short glorious one that is promised to him on the plains of Troy.

This makes the last words of the Declaration most remarkable of all—the signers pledge their lives, their fortunes, and notably their "*sacred Honor*." In effect, they proclaimed that they were willing to lose their lives and fortunes—already extraordinary enough – and, if need be, their "sacred honor" as well. This statement remains a bit mysterious and incomprehensible, even eliciting such nonsensical responses such as that by an owner of one copy of the Declaration, Norman Lear. In an

thoroughgoing "self-interest properly understood" (*DA* II.ii.8, 500–01). See also Sharon Krause, *Liberalism With Honor* (Cambridge, MA: Harvard University Press, 2002).

11 Ancient Greek portrayals of the afterlife were almost without exception dismal and horrific. See, for example, Book 11 of the *Odyssey*, in which Odysseus must slit the throat of a ram and empty its blood into a trough, which then attracts the spirits of the departed who are desperate to drink the vile brew. Incapable of speech—except when they have drunk the blood—and insubstantial, most of the spirits to whom Odysseus speaks bemoan their existence, including, most famously, Achilles, who wishes that he were a slave above the surface rather than to be king of all the dead.

interview with Bill Moyers, Lear was asked what he thought the phrase "sacred honor" meant. Lear replied, "I think sacred honor means if I say it to you, count on me, you can count on me . . . . If I say I'll be there, if I say you matter to me, you can count on it," and compared it to the dedication that the family showed to each other in *The Godfather*.[12] Lear is correct in one sense—the signers were pledging their honor to each other, pledging to stay true to their word and to maintain their unanimity even in the hard times ahead—but he misses the point that in this concluding sentence (as do most who spare the time to reflect on the peroration), they are also stating what they are willing to give up. In pledging their lives and fortunes, they express their willingness to lose each or both in the course of their revolution against Britain. The meaning in the case of a pledge of one's "sacred honor" is all the more extraordinary: following a statement of their willingness to sacrifice their lives and fortunes, the signers also express a willingness to offer up even their sacred honor. But to give up their honor—for the sake of securing independence—is an awesome and chilling statement.

Imagine, for a moment, what it would mean to accept the prospect of losing one's "sacred honor." As schoolchildren growing up in Connecticut, we were constantly reminded in particular about two native figures. One was a hero about whom all of us were taught to be extremely proud—Nathan Hale. We would be taken on field trips to his homestead in Coventry and we were asked (or forced) to memorize his famous last words that he spoke as the hangman's noose was fitted around his neck by the British: "I only regret that I have but one life to lose for my country." We honored Nathan Hale by calling him a war hero, by visiting his homestead and pondering his statue, by remembering him with admiration and some awe.

The other figure we learned of about the same time was Benedict Arnold—a man whose name, like Judas or Brutus, has come to be synonymous with the word "traitor." We did not take field trips to his birthplace in Norwich, though that would have been closer to my home town; there is no "Benedict Arnold Homestead" to visit, in fact. We learned

---

12 "Bill Moyers Interviews Norman Lear" at http://www.pbs.org/now/transcript/transcript_lear.html.

that he was a traitor, someone who offered to surrender West Point to the British for 20,000 pounds. To this day, we treat him with dishonor by calling someone whom we have trusted, and who has betrayed us, a "Benedict Arnold." Nevertheless, according to the "objective" ledger of history, Benedict Arnold was a significant general without whom the American side might have lost the war early on, while Nathan Hale was a failed spy. Nonetheless, as a schoolchild in Connecticut, there was always no question whom one should more admire.

And yet, had the war gone differently—had the British won the war, and had we remained subjects of the British crown—there are fairly good odds that as a child I would have visited the Homestead of the hero Benedict Arnold and we might possibly have called those who had betrayed "us" a "Nathan Hale" or a "John Adams" or a "George Washington." That's the nature (or, absence of nature) of honor—it is not something that is accorded solely to an act itself (one can honor the acts of a spy like Nathan Hale, after all) or to the actor himself, but something that is *given by* other people who themselves determine what is deserving of honor. At various times in human history the same action and the same actor have been alternatively praised or blamed—such as Brutus, whose name sometimes means "traitor" as much as "Judas" or "Benedict Arnold," and who was put in the ninth circle of Hell by Dante for betraying a friend for the sake of his country—whereas sometimes, especially in republican eras, Brutus is held out as a paramount example of civic courage and accorded every honor. So honor is to significant extent in the "eye of the beholder," a fickle legacy on which to stake one's life, or, better put, on which to be willing to stake one's life.

And yet, when one is willing to give up one's fortune and one's life, one might reasonably hope for a place of honor in the hearts and memory of one's countrymen. But the signers of the Declaration were altogether aware that they were putting their own "sacred honor" as much on the line as their wealth and their survival. They knew that in the event of defeat, their reputations would be sullied and subsequent generations would view them with dishonor and contempt.

On Independence Day we honor these men, and all the patriots (see my use of language?—patriots, not "traitors") who risked *everything* for the sake of political independence. Yet, because we now honor them, we sometimes overlook the extent of their willingness to sacrifice. Since we see all too easily the actual sacrifices they made in "fortunes" and "life," we can easily miss the significance of their willingness to sacrifice the honor that we gladly now accord them. And for that same reason, we can easily miss how essential that form of sacrifice that was not finally demanded of them—a loss of their "sacred honor"—remains an essential kind of sacrifice that all democratic citizens have to be willing to make. Over the years, and with intervening heroes to honor, like Abraham Lincoln and Martin Luther King—we tend to see most clearly the willingness to sacrifice one's *life*, and lose sight of that even more incredible, and unfathomable willingness to lose one's honor. To make those sacrifices more sensible—to continue to put the clothes of "self-sacrifice" on the liberal body of "self-interest" and "self-preservation"— we continue to place a high regard on honor, and all too easily lose sight of the ultimate civic courage that may be called upon from time to time that threatens even the expectation of honor's reception as a legacy of self-sacrifice.

The Hard Discipline of Democratic Citizenship

The willingness to sacrifice honor for the sake of a democratic polity is extraordinary, and those citizens who have taken that risk, and have succeeded in their endeavor, are duly honored. They are honored perhaps insufficiently, since the extent of their willingness to sacrifice—even their honor—is largely underacknowledged. Perhaps equally unacknowledged in this reconsideration of the nature of democratic virtue (or one aspect, at least), is the extent to which such recognition relies upon the cultivated capacity of the *citizenry* to recognize acts that are praiseworthy, and hence proper objects of honor. This is the point of William James's remarkable praise of the civil war hero Robert Gould Shaw—not that he deserved our honor, for certainly he was receiving that at the moment James was delivering his speech before the newly unveiled statue of Shaw and his regiment on the Boston Commons—but, rather, that democratic citizens sufficiently and properly conceive of those actions that are honorable. Such actions, in James's view, were not always readily perceptible, and subject to oversight amid the flamboyant actions that can be perceived through the more immediate sense of sight, rather the more philosophic and democratic faculties of hearing and speaking (one thinks here, for example, of the military prowess of Alcibiades compared to the quiet persistence of Socrates, in both military and civic life).

Hence, James attempts the bold act of reassessing the contributions of Shaw in front of a crowd of civil war veterans. Robert Gould Shaw, of course, was the Union colonel during the Civil War of the 54th Massachusetts regiment. He was portrayed by Matthew Broderick in the movie "Glory." This monument erected to Shaw and the men of the 54th—the first African-American regiment of the North—is a marvelous work that still stands in the Boston Commons. Shaw is depicted on horseback facing stoically forward, and his men march silently beside him, with backpacks and rolled sleeping bags and muskets loaded on their backs. They face south, and above them flies a winged female figure, an angel of vengeance perhaps, except that she holds an olive branch in her hand. They are warriors who seek to make peace, the sculptor Saint-Gaudens suggested.

The movie "Glory" portrays Robert Shaw with many (figurative) warts, including his sometimes impatience with his men and his sometimes uncertainty of their ability to fight in the coming battles. But the movie portrays him quite heroically as well, and that is appropriate, since he did meet a hero's death with nearly half his regiment during the attack of heavily fortified Fort Wagner on July 18, 1863. But to the extent that the movie doesn't portray Shaw in all of his complexity, we miss a certain kind of heroism that marked his life that is otherwise easily obscured by the more obvious battlefield heroism that is shown in the film's culminating scenes (again, those most visually appealing acts of heroism).

It's instructive to go back and read about Shaw's life and through some of the many letters he sent to his family over the years.[13] Shaw was

---

13   I have benefited especially by consultation of *Blue-Eyed Child of Fortune: The Civil War Letters of Colonel Robert Gould Shaw*, ed. by Russell Duncan (Athens, GA: The University of Georgia Press, 1992); and *Hope and Glory: Essays on the Legacy of the Fifty-fourth Massachusetts Regiment*, ed. by Martin H. Blatt, Thomas J. Brown and Donald Yacovone (Amherst, MA: The University of Massachusetts Press, 2001).

the child of privilege—he grew up in one of the most prominent and wealthy Boston families of the time, and was educated privately at schools in New York City, in Switzerland and Germany, and finally at Harvard. And yet, for all this, he was— for lack of a better word—something of a slacker. He loved to party, and had a particularly good time while he was away from his parents while at boarding school in Germany. In one letter home he wrote, "all I can say is that I have not taste for anything except amusing myself."[14] He spent money wantonly on gambling, drink and entertainment, and in the words of one biographer, he "partied with abandon." In one of my favorite letters, he describes to his mother that there were fifteen English girls boarding nearby in Hannover, Germany, and, because they went to church every Sunday, he wrote, "I am beginning to go too."[15]

Shaw was rebelling against parents who were, basically, "do-gooders." They were renowned for their interest in reform, and gained particular prominence in abolitionist circles of Boston—which is saying quite a bit, since Boston was one of the centers of abolitionism. He was seeking to simply have a good time without having to think about saving the world, it seemed—and let his parents know it in his letters home. In one he summed up this sentiment by writing, "I don't want to become a reformer, Apostle, or anything of the kind, there is no use in doing disagreeable things for nothing."[16]

Yet, with the attack on Fort Sumter in 1860, Shaw was among the first to sign up—then for the New York regiment that reached Washington D.C. first in those tense days when the capitol had no military defense, deep in the heart of Dixie—and eventually rose to become a colonel in the Massachusetts Second regiment, one of the premier regiments during the Civil War. In 1863, as the war became increasingly perceived as one of liberty and equality and not exclusively Union, a move to use African-American soldiers was set into motion, among others by the Governor of Massachusetts, John Andrew. Lincoln eventually approved of this proposal, and Andrew offered Robert Gould Shaw the

---

14 Joan Waugh, "It Was a Sacrifice We Owed," in *Hope and Glory*, 63.
15 Russell Duncan, "Introduction," *Blue-Eyed Child of Fortune*, 9–10.
16 Joan Waugh, "It Was a Sacrifice We Owed," in *Hope and Glory*, 63.

command of the 54th Massachusetts—the first Northern regiment made up completely of black infantry. The movie portrays Shaw's hesitation as lasting minutes, but in fact Shaw initially declined the commission in order to remain with the Massachusetts 2nd. While he did not articulate his motivations for this initial decision, he had many friends in the 2nd— and many of them did not altogether approve of the 54th. He knew his chances of advancement in the 2nd were very good, and that he stood to lose much by taking command of an unproven regiment that many people were watching and waiting to fail. He recognized that the only reason to accept the commission was out of duty—and, at that, primarily duty to the wishes of his parents. As he wrote to his fiancée, "If I had taken it [the Fifty-fourth colonelcy], it would only have been from a sense of duty. I am afraid Mother will think I am shirking my duty."[17] It took several days for Shaw to change his mind, and once he accepted the commission he never really looked back, though from time to time he did wish himself still a member of the 2nd—particularly after its role in the Union victory at Gettysburg.

Arguably, it is *this* decision of Robert Gould Shaw—to take command of the 54th—that deserves at least as much attention as his final, very brave decision to lead the charge, almost certainly to his death, against Fort Wagner. To see this decision in all its clarity, it's helpful to jump ahead 34 years to May 31, 1897, when the monument to Shaw and the 54th was dedicated on the Boston Commons. Among the speakers that day was William James—whose brother, Willkie, was a lieutenant in the 54th—whose speech reminds us of how important that decision was.

In his address, James suggested that Shaw's form of military heroism was not the most admirable form of virtue necessary for citizens in a democratic republic. While he praised Shaw's military valor, he found even more praiseworthy what he called Shaw's form of "lonely" or "civic" courage that Shaw exhibited when he resigned his "warm commission in the glorious Second" in order assume the more "dubious" command of the "negroes of the Fifty-fourth." In a stirring passage, James went on,

17   Joan Waugh, "It Was a Sacrifice We Owed," in *Hope and Glory*, 67.

That lonely kind of courage (civic courage as we call it in peace-times) is the kind of valor to which the monuments of nations should most of all be reared, for the survival of the fittest has not bred it into the bone of human beings as it has bred military valor; and of five hundred of us who could storm a battery side by side with others, perhaps not one could be found who would risk his worldly fortunes all alone in resisting an enthroned abuse.

A democratic republic would not ultimately be saved by such acts of military valor, James went on, but rather "by acts without external picturesqueness; by speaking, writing, voting reasonably; by smiting corruption swiftly; by good temper between parties; by the people knowing true men when they see them, and preferring them as leaders to rabid partisans or empty quacks."

James turns tradition on its head: honor is owed to citizens of extraordinary civic courage—not that more "common" virtue of military bravery viewed since antiquity until contemporary times instead as an "extraordinary" virtue. What James points to is that willingness to sacrifice, first and foremost, not one's life—which, he says, is comparatively far easier— but one's honor, one's place of esteem in the eyes of others, the kind of recognition that even those who have sacrificed their lives can expect.

By means of his allusion to Darwinism, James apparently suggests that such "ordinary virtue" is altogether unexpected, only infrequently to be found among the mass of humanity since "the survival of the fittest has not bred it into the bone of human beings as it has bred military valor." Yet, in his description of its homely form—expressed in mundane political forms like voting, deliberating, and judgment—such virtue is nonetheless expected to be widespread. Such virtue is not the result of "nature," but of cultivation and civic education.[18] That which is

18 James was deeply skeptical about the claims of Social Darwinism. See, for example, his letter to the editor of the *Nation* which argued that such "scientific" theory was nothing more than a form of "faith": "The Mood of Science and the Mood of Faith" (1874), *Essays, Comments and Reviews*.

apparently most rare must be altogether common in a democracy; the extraordinary must become ordinary.

James points to the extraordinary nature of this form of civic courage by noting that it is a form of virtue for which monuments *ought* to be erected; thus, he alerts his audience to the fact that such virtue rarely if ever receives similar honor as that accorded to military valor. Honors are more easily accorded to "picturesque" acts and deeds of striking nobility and obvious sacrifice, rather than those acts that are born of quiet perseverance, silent cooperation, muffled nobility, and, at times, a stolid willingness to forego the marks of honor in defense of that which is perceived wrongly to be dishonorable. Of course, the fact that James was delivering this address before a group of veterans (including Oliver Wendell Holmes, who bore the bodily and philosophical scars of severe wounds) from a war in which he did not serve only underlined his boldness in making this argument.[19]

James points to a paradox: civic virtue, particularly that rare willingness among democratic citizens to act quietly or speak out loudly against immoral prevailing beliefs or unjust practices, ought to be honored, but—and here's the problem— *by definition* they cannot be so

The Works of William James, 115–17 [after expressing his skepticism about Huxley's social Darwinism, James delightfully signs the letter, "Ignoramus" (117)]. James's most explicit call for a form of civic education supportive of democracy is found in the same volume in his essay "The Social Value of the College-Bred" (1907), in which he asserts that "democracy is a kind of religion, and we are bound not to admit its failure. Faiths and utopias are the noblest exercise of human reason, and no one with a spark of reason in him will sit down fatalistically before the croaker's picture" (109).

19 This point is succinctly emphasized in the following comment on James's speech:

James's slap at American militarism, delivered from a stage crowded with fifty former or present officers, including his old debating opponent Wendell Holmes, in itself required no small measure of the civic courage he praised in Shaw.

Thomas J. Brown, "Reconstructing Boston: Civil Monuments of the Civil War," in *Hope and Glory*, 154.

honored, at least not at the time that such civic courage against popular perceptions is displayed. Shaw's supreme sacrifice on the battlefield is immediately recognizable for its honorableness, but less immediately recognizable is the praiseworthy action of assuming command of a "dubious" regiment composed of "inferior" soldiers. While James rightly points out that such actions are perhaps more deserving of honor – given that they are undertaken with disregard for, and often in direct conflict with, what is normally held to be honorable—he recognizes implicitly that this cannot be the case. One cannot immediately honor that which a polity does not recognize as honorable, thus making such a form of "civic courage" all the more extraordinary. Apparently praising a form of virtue that is quite "ordinary" in comparison to the more "picturesque" courage of a fallen soldier, James indicates that such "ordinary virtue" is in fact quite extraordinary, and particularly—even especially so—in a democracy.

James here echoes a concern that had been brilliantly articulated 62 years earlier (and 27 years before Shaw took the command of the 54th) by Alexis de Tocqueville. In *Democracy in America*, published first in 1835, Tocqueville expressed what he called a "religious terror" at the prospects for democracy in the modern world—he was at once of the view that it was unstoppable, a human development being directed by nothing less than Divine Providence itself, and yet that it contained tendencies that might prove ultimately destructive to the human liberty and equality that democracy rightly trumpeted.[20] Primary among those aspects of democracy that concerned him was the prospect of the rise of a new form of despotism that threatened to arise from the apparently benign form of self-government practiced in democracy. Famously, he called this new form of despotism "Tyranny of the Majority."

Tocqueville believed that political resistance was possible in ancient democracies because of the smaller *size* of those regimes (one could more easily dismiss a majority because one knew the individuals that made up that majority, and hence knew the quirks that lie behind those numbers); and that aristocracies did not follow popular opinion because of a strong sense of privilege and rank. But in modern mass democracies,

---

20 Tocqueville, *Democracy in America*, "Introduction," 6.

neither of these conditions applied: individuals who saw themselves in opposition could only perceive the majority as a faceless mass, and increasingly did not have appeals outside those sanctioned by democracy itself—namely, rule of the majority. Tocqueville described "tyranny of the majority" to be, by and large, a *psychological* condition in which each democratic individual feared, above all, to be perceived as differing from the views of the mass. He even went so far as to suggest that such fear made people less free than even the fear of physical pain and death threatened by princes of previous ages. He wrote that

> Chains and executioners are the coarse instruments that tyranny formerly employed; but in our day civilization has perfected even despotism itself, which seemed, indeed, to have nothing more to learn. Princes had so to speak made violence material; democratic republics in our day have rendered it just as intellectual as the human will that it was intended to constrain. Under the absolute government of one alone, despotism struck the body crudely, so as to reach the soul; and the soul, escaping from those blows, rose gloriously above it; but in democratic republics, tyranny does not proceed in this way; it leaves the body and goes straight for the soul. The master no longer says to it: You shall think as I do or you shall die; he says: You are free not to think as I do; your life, your goods, everything remains to you; but from this day on, you are a stranger among us . . . . Go in peace, I leave you your life, but I leave it to you worse than death.[21]

Thinking themselves free because their *bodies* are not threatened, Tocqueville feared that democratic citizens might become *less* free over time by internalizing the desire not to be ostracized by the many, not to be on the wrong side of an essential question—instead, to use Emerson's phrase, it was easier to "go with the flow," and to avoid being caught in a "landslide," to use the quaint electoral term. He saw this "internalization"

---

21 Tocqueville, *Democracy in America*, I.ii.7, p. 244–45.

of avoidance taking particularly dangerous forms in a democracy—especially in the form of a desire to escape public life altogether and instead find dignity in the more intimate circles of private life—in family of an increasingly nuclear variety—and in private business where one might hope to be rewarded materially and not run the risk of provoking disapproval. He wrote that the democratic individual was in danger, over time, of being "thrown back on himself alone," and of finally being "shut up in the solitude of his own heart."[22]

Ironically, this very kind of isolation would make the "lonely courage" of the sort exhibited by Robert Shaw more difficult. We may praise the Shaws, or the Thoreaus or Emersons or Martin Luther Kings for their "lonely" courage, but theirs was a singular courage that was not enacted alone. Each had extensive networks of friends and family supporting them, shoring their belief that their cause was right even in the face of popular disapproval. Moreover, each saw the central importance of acting in *public*—the need to act politically, to stand up against popular opinion on vitally important questions of the day and not choose the temptation of withdrawal to the comfort and ease of private life. And for each of these "extraordinary acts," democracy needs a hundred-fold the smaller and far less visible acts of "ordinary virtue" described by William James—"speaking, writing, voting reasonably; by smiting corruption swiftly; by good temper between parties; by the people knowing true men when they see them." These emblems of "ordinary virtue"— ones from which we can expect little honor and sometimes can receive intense dishonor—are the forms of everyday civic virtue that democracy requires, and without which cannot persist.

All the great virtues—ones that Aristotle argued would be only cultivated among a select group of exceptional men, the *kaloskagathoi*, or "gentlemen"—must needs become "ordinary" in democratic times. One could easily explore the ways in which courage, magnanimity, liberality, indeed, the quality of being "great-souled" are all necessary in extraordinary measure among ordinary citizens. But, perhaps it all comes back to honor, since to honor is necessarily to know what is honorable, and is therefore to reflect those qualities and human features that we find

---

22 Tocqueville, *Democracy in America*, II.ii.2, p. 484.

praiseworthy, and hence which serve as a mirror by which we measure our own accomplishments and shortcomings. It is therefore meet that we honor those extraordinary citizens who have gone before us—those like the signers of the Declaration, or Robert Gould Shaw, who offered, and indeed sacrificed, their fortune and their lives. But amid this bestowal of honor, we ought not to neglect to honor them—however paradoxical it may seem—for their willingness to forego honor, since that is perhaps the greatest sacrifice that a citizen can offer to his fellow citizens—the willingness to forego their admiration on behalf of what is right. On the inscription of the monument dedicated to Robert Shaw and the men of the 54th is a Latin inscription that reads, "Omnia relinquit servare republicam"—"He gave up everything to preserve the Republic." It is the motto of the society of Cincinnatus, who was a Roman soldier. Legend has it that he had retired to a small farm, when at a time of terrible crisis the Republic voted to give him powers of Dictator. He was told by messengers who found him plowing his fields. He took command of the Roman corps and after 16 days of victories, retired again to his fields, relinquishing his position and title. He was honored by the Romans for his singular desire to avoid honor, and it is this kind of honor that Republics must keep alive.

But this is perhaps not the greatest monument in honor of the memory of Robert Shaw. Instead, perhaps that monument that recalls Shaw's willingness to forego honor for the sake of the republic and the equality for which he fought is to be found in several lines of an otherwise forgotten poem written in his honor and commemorating his accomplishments. The poem concludes not in commemoration of his greatest deeds, but rather in recollection of the mass grave of Shaw and his fallen comrades under the ramparts of Fort Wagner; written by William Moody, it concludes,

> They swept, and died like freeman on the height,
> Like freemen, and like men of noble breed;
> And when the battle fell away at night
> By hasty and contemptuous hands were thrust
> Obscurely in a common grave with him
> The fair-haired keeper of their love and trust.

Now limb doth mingle with dissolved limb
In nature's busy old democracy.[23]

To celebrate our final obscurity—the final equality that awaits us all in the end—is to remind ourselves that honor is due to each of us who lives in the shadow of death, nobly plowing our fields, ready to heed the call of the city, even relinquishing our claim to honor as a way of bestowing honor on our fellow citizens and ourselves.

This chapter is a revised version of a speech originally delivered at the New Jersey Governor's School in July 2001. I would like to thank Susan McWilliams for the invitation, and the students and faculty in attendance. Some of the informality of this essay reflects its origin as a speech to an excellent group of high school students.

23   William Moody, "An Ode in Time of Hesitation," l. 112–17.

Chapter 4
Awakening from the American Dream:
The End of Escape in American Cinema?

The Dream of Escape

"What, then, is the American, this new man?" The question, posed in 1782 by the French aristocrat turned Pennsylvania farmer Hector St. John de Crèvecoeur, answers itself: the American is a new man, a creature yet unseen, unknown in the annals of history. He is a being *defined* by his newness—self-created, unbound, indefinable. It is the newness of this new man that astounds Crèvecoeur: "*He* is an American, who, leaving behind him all his ancient prejudices and manners, receives new ones from the new mode of life he has embraced . . . . Here individuals of all nations are melted into a new race of men, whose labours and posterity will one day cause great changes in the world . . . .The American is a new man, who acts upon new principles; he must therefore entertain new ideas and form new opinions."[1] The American sheds all that once defined him in an old and intentionally forgotten world. Most promising, perhaps, is the fact that reinvention does not cease upon arrival in the new world, but remains an ever-present possibility as long as new avenues of escape from the limits and impositions of both the Old and New Worlds alike remain available to the New Man. And, for Crèvecoeur, it is precisely that possibility of escape to new potentials, new freedoms, and new self-definitions that stands so invitingly and inexhaustibly in the American's future: "we are the most perfect society now existing in the

---

1   J. Hector St. John de Crèvecoeur, *Letters from an American Farmer* (New York: Penguin Books, 1983), 69; 70.

world. Here man is free as he ought to be, nor is this pleasing equality so transitory as many others are. Many ages will not see the shores of our great lakes replenished with inland nations, nor the unknown bounds of North America entirely peopled. Who can tell how far it extends? Who can tell the millions of men whom it will feed and contain? For no European foot has as yet traveled half the extent of this mighty continent!"[2]

It should little surprise that a people who left various native lands seeking a new start should define itself as a nation seeking ever-new avenues of re-creation. It is a part of the American soul, a creed in its national devotions as old as its first moments and captured indelibly by some of its ablest spokesmen. At the moment of America's direst early crisis, self-creation became part of America's official national definition as described by Thomas Jefferson in his 1774 pamphlet to a despised King. In "A Summary View of the Rights of Americans," Jefferson recalled that "our ancestors, before their emigration to America, were the free inhabitants of the British dominions in Europe, and possessed a right which nature has given to all men, of departing from the country in which chance, not choice, has placed them, of going in quest of new habitations, and of there establishing new societies, under such laws and regulations as to them shall seem most likely to promote public happiness."[3] Inasmuch as all humans are born into circumstances not of their own choosing, Jefferson proposed a revolutionary new justification for universal mobility, the desire for infinite improvement of circumstance, and a presumed suspicion for those who accepted their unbidden circumstance without reflection and choice. Jefferson in revolutionary prose articulated what untold millions of subsequent Americans would cite as their rationale for "pulling up stakes," "moving out," "starting over," "leaving town," and any countless numbers of less articulate but implicitly theorized declarations of independence from accidental circumstance and a dedication to a life in the pursuit of happiness, in a

---

2   Crèvecoeur, 67–68.
3   Thomas Jefferson, "A Summary View of the Rights of British America," in *Thomas Jefferson: Writings* (New York: Library of America, 1984), 105–06.

place and with people selected purposively and only as long one's own satisfaction with those circumstances warranted.

Always searching for the better choice of locale and the preferable option of lifestyle, this restless quality of the American character thereby also threatened tranquility of mind, undermined stability in communities, and gave rise to the possibility of the perpetually unsatiated soul: happiness pursued, after all, may preclude happiness achieved. Alexis de Tocqueville identified a universal "restlessness" as one of the central characteristics of the American psyche some fifty years after Jefferson's articulation of the right to uproot oneself, and discerned the oppression in spirit that one's infinite physical and psychic freedom could entail. Dreaming constantly of "the goods they do not have," Americans "show themselves constantly tormented by a vague fear of not having chosen the shortest route that can lead to [them]." Tocqueville perceived that the American constantly reaches for the next best thing, exhibits perpetual discontent with what he has achieved and thus "grasps them all without clutching them, and he soon allows them to escape from his hands so as to run after new enjoyments." Rather than achieving ever greater levels of bliss with each perceptible improvement in circumstance, Tocqueville described a people in the throes of a kind of frenzied dissatisfaction: "In addition to the goods that he possesses, at each instant he imagines a thousand others that death will prevent him from enjoying if he does not hasten. This thought fills him with troubles, fears, and regrets, and keeps his soul in a sort of unceasing trepidation that brings him to change his designs and his place at every moment."[4]

Tocqueville identifies a terrible contradiction in the American soul: in their unique craving for "newness," for the infinite possibility of the better, greater, more perfect opportunity, Americans are impelled to pursue a happiness ever out of reach. Incapable of rest and satisfaction with what they have achieved, in effect Americans fall into a form of enslavement – enslavement to a pursuit without end. In their "restlessness" they are endlessly driven without hope of contentment. Unable to restrain their desire for the promise of what lies around the next corner, they

4   Alexis de Tocqueville, *Democracy in America*, trans. Harvey C. Mansfield and Delba Winthrop (Chicago: University of Chicago Press, 2000).

prove unable to find satisfaction with what they have come to know on their own street. The imperative of choice removes the choice to rest, to declare the search over, to accept limits, dissatisfactions, imperfections, impingements, discomfort, humiliations, and in turn to overlook satisfaction, fulfillment, ease, familiarity, friendship, community, and happiness. By declaring what he is not, the American precludes discovering what he is; by insisting on what he will not have, he prevents himself from keeping anything.

What follows is an analysis of three popular films ranging from the 1940s to the 1990s. Each captures an aspect of this ingrained feature of American character, the dream of escape. In *It's a Wonderful Life*, we witness the endearing story of George Bailey, a man who desperately craves to escape the limiting life of the small town of Bedford Falls. *Avalon* points to the cost of realizing escape, particularly the loss of community, and with it the loss of collective memory, a loss that leads to the triumph of amnesia over memorial for the dead. Lastly, *American Beauty* portrays the fruits of escape, the entrapment of the modern bourgeois American, and yet suggests a new form of escape in the rejection of the traditional American dream of escape, a form of escape that, ironically, only further embraces the solipsistic trajectory of American escape.

It's a Destructive Life

Frank Capra's "It's A Wonderful Life" portrays the decent life of a small-town American, George Bailey (Jimmy Stewart), an everyman who saves his community from an evil Scrooge—Henry F. Potter (Lionel Barrymore)—and who only comes to realize his accomplishments by witnessing what terrors might have occurred had he never lived. George Bailey represents all that is good and decent about America: a family man beloved by his community for his kindness and generosity.

Yet, if there is a dark side of America, the film quite ably captures that aspect as well—and contrary to popular belief, it is found not solely in Mr. Potter. One sees a dark side represented by George Bailey himself: the optimist, the adventurer, the builder, the man who deeply hates the town that gives him sustenance, who craves nothing else but to get out of Bedford Falls and remake the world. Given its long-standing reputation as a nostalgic look at small-town life in the pre-war period, it is almost shocking to suggest that the film is one of the most potent, if unconscious critiques ever made of the American dream that was so often hatched in this small-town setting. For George Bailey, in fact, destroys the town that saves him in the end.

Undoubtedly viewers have come to adore this film in part because it portrays what Americans intuitively sense they have lost. Among the film's first scenes is the portrayal of an idyllic Bedford Falls covered in freshly fallen snow, people strolling on sidewalks, a few cars meandering slowly along the streets, numerous small stores stretching down each side of the tree-lined streets. It is an America increasingly unknown and unseen: wounded first by Woolworth, then K-Mart, then Wal-Mart; mercilessly bled by the automobile; drained of life by subdivisions, interstates, and the suburbs. Americans admire this movie because it portrays Mr. Gower's drug store as a place to meet neighbors over a soda or an ice cream, not merely a place to be treated as a faceless consumer buying an endless variety of pain-killers; similarly, like Cheers, Martini's bar is somewhere everybody knows your name, a place to spend a few minutes with friends after work before one walks home.

George Bailey hates this town. Even as a child, he wants to escape its limiting clutches, ideally to visit the distant and exotic locales vividly pictured in *National Geographic*. As he grows, his ambitions change in a significant direction: he craves "to build things, design new buildings, plan modern cities." The modern city of his dreams is imagined in direct contrast to the enclosure of Bedford Falls: it is to be open, fast, glittering, kaleidoscopic. He craves "to shake off the dust of this crummy little town" to build "airfields, skyscrapers onc hundred stories tall, bridges a mile long . . . ." George represents the vision of post-war America: the ambition to alter the landscape so as to accommodate modern life, to uproot nature and replace it with monuments of human accomplishment, to re-engineer life for mobility and swiftness, one unencumbered by permanence, one no longer limited to a moderate and comprehensible human scale.

George's great dreams are thwarted by innumerable circumstances of fate and accident: most of the film portrays a re-telling of various episodes of George's life for the benefit of a guardian angel—Clarence

Oddbody (Henry Travers)—who will shortly be sent down to earth to attempt to save George during his greatest test. Despite all of George's many attempts to leave the town of Bedford Falls—first as a young man with plans to travel to Europe, later to college, and then still later, and more modestly, to New York City, various intervening events constantly prevent George from even once leaving Bedford Falls. In the course of relating his life, however, we discover that George has helped innumerable people in the community over the years; these countless seemingly small interventions it will be later discovered to have amounted to the salvation of the entire town. Despite George's persistent desire to escape the limitations of life in Bedford Falls, George becomes a stalwart citizen of the town he otherwise claims to despise.

However, if George's grandiose designs, first to become an explorer, and later to build new modern cities, are thwarted due to bad fortune, he does not cease to be ambitious, and does not abandon the dream of transforming America, even if his field of design is narrowed. Rather, his ambitions are channeled into the only available avenue that life and his position now offer: he creates not airfields nor skyscrapers nor modern cities, but remakes Bedford Falls itself. His efforts are portrayed as nothing less than noble: he creates "Bailey Park," a modern subdivision of single-family houses, thus allowing hundreds of citizens of Bedford Falls to escape the greedy and malignant clutches of Mr. Potter, who gouges these families in the inferior rental slums of "Pottersville." George's efforts are portrayed as altogether praiseworthy, and it is right to side with him against the brutal and heartless greed of Potter. However, such sympathies serve also to obscure the nature of Bailey's activities, and their ultimate consequences. In particular, it is worth observing the nature of "Bailey Park," not merely by contrast to "Pottersville"—in comparison to which it is clearly superior—but also in contrast to downtown Bedford Falls, where it may not compare as favorably by some estimations.

Bedford Falls has an intimate town center, and blocks of houses with front porches where people leisurely sit and greet passersby who constantly amble on the nearby sidewalks. Bedford Falls is a town with a deep sense of place and history. When George's car crashes into a tree, the owner berates him for the gash he has made: "My great-grandfather planted this tree," he says. He is the fourth generation to live in his house, and the tree's presence serves as a living link to his ancestors, a symbol of the stories told about the dead to the living and to the unborn.

It is especially worth noting the significant role of the front porch in the course of the film. Numerous scenes take place in the intermediate space between home and street. While apparently serving as a backdrop for the more obvious action on the screen, it is worth pausing to consider the contributions, even "role," of the porch in the underlying assumptions about a way of life that Bedford Falls permits. In a discerning essay entitled "From Porch to Patio," Richard H. Thomas notes that the front porch—built in part for functional purposes, especially in order to provide an outdoor space that could be used to cool off during the summer—also served a host of social functions as well: a place of "trivial greetings," a spot from which an owner could invite a passerby to stop for conversation in an informal setting, a space where "courting" could take place within earshot of parents or the elderly could take in the sights and sounds of passing life around them, the porch "facilitated and symbolized a set of social relationships and the strong bond of community feeling which people during the nineteenth century supposed was the way God intended life to be lived."[5]

By contrast, Bailey Park has no trees, no sidewalks, and no porches. It is a modern subdivision: the trees have been plowed under to make room for wide streets and large yards with garages. Compared to Bedford Falls—which is always filled with strolling people—the development is empty, devoid of human presence. The residents of this modern development are presumably hidden behind the doors of their modern houses, or, if outside, relaxing in back on their patios. The absence of front porches suggests an alternative conception of life that will govern Bailey Park—life is to be led in private, not in the intermediate public spaces in front that link the street to the home. One doubts that anyone will live in these houses for four generations, much less one. The absence of informal human interaction in Bailey Park stands in gross contrast to the vibrancy of Bedford Falls.

5   Richard H. Thomas, "From Porch to Patio," *The Palimpsest* (August, 1995): 123.

The patio—successor to the front porch—embodies as many implicit assumptions about how life is to be led as the porch. Thomas notes the move from urban centers into suburban enclaves in the years following World War II led to the creation of "bedroom communities" in which one did not know one's neighbors and where frequent turnover made such stable community relationships unlikely, where privacy and safety were dual concerns leading to the creation of the "patio" space *behind* the house, most often at the expense of a porch in the front. As Thomas contrasts the two,

> "the patio is an extension of the house, but far less public than the porch. It was easy to greet a stranger from the porch but exceedingly difficult to do so from the backyard patio . . . . The old cliché says, 'A man's home is his castle. If this be true, the nineteenth-century porch was a drawbridge across which many passed in their daily lives. The modern patio is in many ways a closed courtyard that suggests that the king and his family are tired of the world and seek only the companionship of their immediate family or peers."[6]

Bailey Park is not simply a community that will grow to have a similar form of life and communal interaction as Bedford Falls; instead, George Bailey's grand social experiment in progressive living represents a fundamental break from the way of life in Bedford Falls, from a stable and interactive community to a more nuclear and private collection of households who will find in Bailey Park shelter but little else in common.[7]

---

6 Thomas, 126–27.
7 People in such communities cease to lead a common life, but increasingly share common *interests* that are based on similar socio-economic backgrounds. Such self-selected "communities" result in a decline of interaction between people of different classes, backgrounds, ethnicities, and experience, even as it gives the outward *appearance* of commonality through concurrence of interests. See Robert B. Reich, "The Politics of Secession," in *Work of Nations* (New York: Vintage Books, 1992), 282–300; and Christopher Lasch, *The Revolt of the Elites and the Betrayal of Democracy* (New York: W. W. Norton & Co., 1995), 25–49.

We also learn something far more sinister about Bailey Park toward the end of the film. George contemplates suicide after his Uncle has misplaced $8,000 and George comes under a cloud of suspicion. At this point the recounting of George's life for the benefit of Clarence the angel ends, and Clarence enters the action to dissuade George from taking his life. Inspired by George's lament that it would have been better had he never lived, Clarence grants his wish—he shows what life in Bedford Falls would have been like without the existence of George Bailey. George's many small and large acts of kindness are now seen in their cumulative effect. Particular lives are thoroughly ruined or lost in the absence of George's efforts. Further, the entire town—now called "Pottersville"— is transformed into a seedy, corrupt city in the absence of George's heroic resistance to Potter's greediness.

Attempting to comprehend what has happened, and refusing to believe Clarence's explanations, George attempts to retrace his steps. He recalls that this awful transformation first occurred when he was at Martini's bar, and decides to seek out Martini at home. Martini, in the first reality, is one of the beneficiaries of George's assistance when he is able to purchase a home in Bailey Park; however, in the alternate reality without George, of course the subdivision is never built. Still refusing to believe what has transpired, George makes his way through the forest where Bailey Park *would have been*, but instead ends in front of the town's old cemetery outside town. Facing the old gravestones, Clarence asks, "Are you sure Martini's house is here?" George is dumbfounded: "Yes, it should be." George confirms a horrific suspicion: *Bailey Park has been built atop the old cemetery*. Not only does George raze the trees, but he commits an act of unspeakable sacrilege. He obliterates a sacred symbol of Bedford Fall's connection with the past, the grave markers of the town's ancestors. George Bailey's vision of a modern America eliminates his links with his forebears, covers up the evidence of death, supplies people instead with private retreats of secluded isolation, and all at the expense of an intimate community, in life and in death.

George prays to Clarence to be returned to his previous life, to suffer the consequences of the seeming embezzlement, but to embrace "the wonderful life" he has lived, and has in turn created for others as well. His prayer granted, George returns home to find that a warrant for his arrest awaits him, as well as reporters poised to publicize his shame. However, his wife Mary has contacted those innumerable people whose lives George has touched to tell them of George's plight. In one of the most moving scenes on film, George's neighbors, friends and family come flocking to his house, each contributing what little they can to make up the deficit until a pile of money builds in front of George. Trust runs deep in such a stable community of long-standing relationships: as Uncle Billy exclaims amid the rush of contributors, "they didn't ask any questions, George. They just heard you were in trouble, and they came from every direction." George is saved from prison and obloquy, and Clarence earns the wings he has been awaiting.

Despite the charm of the ending, a nagging question lingers, especially when we consider that many of the neighbors who come to George's rescue are ones who now live in Bailey Park. If the tight-knit community of Bedford Falls makes it possible for George to have built up long-standing trust and commitment with his neighbors over the years, such that they unquestioningly give him money despite the suspicion of embezzlement, will those people who have *only* known life in Bailey Park be likely to do the same for a neighbor who has hit upon hard times? What of the children of those families in Bailey Park, or George's children as they move away from the small-town life of Bedford Falls? A deep irony pervades the film at the moment of it joyous conclusion: as the developer of an antiseptic suburban subdivision, George Bailey is saved through the kinds of relationships nourished in his town that will be undermined and even precluded in the anomic community he builds as an adult.

Nostalgia and the Inescapability of Regret

Barry Levinson's *Avalon* (1991) is both a paean to the cohesive immigrant culture of early twentieth-century Baltimore and a lament for the "lost city" in the wake of the automobile, the suburbs, and television. While acknowledging the temptations, even inevitability of escape in a nation with abundant land and populated by the offspring of the restless spirits who settled it, Levinson indulges in nostalgia for erstwhile networks of extended family, the obligations and trust that such commitments engendered, and the intimacy and slowness of everyday life that allowed for remembrance of the past through story-telling and inherited memory. Yet, while sometimes cloying, the nostalgia never overbears, as Levinson is attentive to all of the limitations that immigrant urban life entailed, including the absence of private space, the resulting fraying of familial nerves, and the unfulfilled cravings for the outward signs of success that post-War Americans increasingly sought to display.

Avalon centers on the story of two generations of the Krichinsky family of Poland. The film opens with the wizened voice of Sam Krichinsky (Armin Mueller-Stahl) telling about the day when he arrived in America. Sam arrives in Baltimore on July 4, 1914, amid the explosions of fireworks, endless red white and blue bunting, and streams of citizens on the streets celebrating with sparklers. We discover that he is telling this story to an entranced group of children on Thanksgiving many decades after his arrival, above the background din of silverware and the complaint of his wife who berates him for telling the story yet again. He continues with his story nevertheless, insisting that "if you stop remembering, you forget." *Avalon* marks the passing of years by successive portrayals of Independence Day and Thanksgiving, unquestionably *the* two most "American" of American holidays, and reveals the transformation of civic and familial structures and practices over time. Independence Day of 1914 could not be portrayed more patriotically, and Thanksgiving several decades later depicted in the film's opening scenes is the occasion for an enormous gathering of extended family who live in a small, even encroaching world of row-houses in Baltimore. Both holidays change markedly with the passing years.

The world of Baltimore in the years preceding World War II is portrayed as settled, predictable, and comfortable. The children of the Krichinsky brothers benefit from this settled world—growing up in close proximity, with two cousins in particular, Gabriel and Izzy (Aidan Quinn and Kevin Pollack) sharing a closeness resembling that of brothers—even as that world after World War II becomes increasingly unsatisfying to the subsequent generation. Gabriel and Izzy work as door-to-door salesmen at the beginning of the film, like their parents, willing to work hard to earn a modest living that allows them to share space with parents and siblings in the crowded row-houses of the old neighborhood. For all

the charms of city living, life there is portrayed as constraining and limiting for the ambitious younger generation. Gabriel's wife Ann (Elizabeth
Perkins) lodges a standing complaint about the overcrowding of the
small row-house which they share with Gabriel's parents, Sam and Eva
Krichinksy, as well as their own son Michael: "The problem is we never
have a moment's privacy. Everyone is on top of everyone; we need our
own place." Izzy and Gabriel—who continue to live across the street
from one another presumably in the houses they grew up in, though now
with their spouses and own children as well as their parents—grow discontent with the limits inherent in this comfortable but confining existence.

This discontent is symbolized most starkly during a flashback as
Sam tells his grandchildren—Michael, as ever, among them—about the
marriages of Gabriel and Izzy. They have both married American women
(not women from their own neighborhoods and similar ethnic backgrounds), opting not for a family wedding but instead eloping without
knowledge and approval of their elders. As Sam reads their marriage li-
censes he discovers that each Krichinsky son has changed his surname
as well—they are now Gabriel Kaye and Izzy Kirk. Sam is furious:
"What are you, a candy bar? How can we be a family?" he asks them.
And although he eventually forgives them, his question lingers—how
can the family persist when its most outward sign, a shared name, the
inherited accident of birth that shows that one belongs to a community
unchosen but inextricably one's own, has been abandoned by intention
and design? Both Gabriel and Izzy join that oldest of American attempts
at escape from the past, the creation of a new identity, the sloughing off
of an unchosen inheritance and arbitrary past for a chosen future, echo-
ing that ancient right claimed by Jefferson when justifying the right of
all people to leave the unchosen home of birth for a chosen place of destination.

Increasingly, *choice* comes to dominate the film, and is shown to be
the natural inheritance of America's immigrant families. The successive
generations merely assume the same right to opt out of their inherited
communities, just as their elders did when they emigrated to America—
but in so doing, they thereby threaten the new communities that were
built as refuges of belonging in the New World. *Avalon* portrays a

Baltimore as lost as the Chicago that Alan Ehrenhalt has described in his seminal study, *The Lost City*, in which he observes that contemporary nostalgia for community often neglects the costs that necessarily accompany the cohesiveness of such settings, primary among which is the *absence* of choice in many aspects of daily life.

> To worship choice and community together is to misunderstand what community is all about. Community means not subjecting every action in life to the burden of choice, but rather accepting the familiar and reaping the psychological benefits of having one less calculation to make in the course of the day.[8]

The old neighborhood is increasingly bombarded by the choices that result from the prosperity of the 1950s, choices that are viewed warily by the older generation even as they are embraced by their children and grandchildren. Detecting and seeking to capitalize on this restlessness and increased craving for the novel, Gabriel and Izzy, having chosen new identities, forswear their careers as door-to-door salesmen and open a store that sells televisions—with numerous different brands and dozens of styles. The logic of choice culminates in their opening of a warehouse department store—now no longer in the center of the city, but at the outskirts, reachable only by automobile, presumably since the lower cost in rent and overhead allows for cheaper prices, greater sales, and ever more expansion of choice as consumer demand and expectations grow. They open their new warehouse store on July 4th, many years after Sam Krichinsky's arrival in America amid the patriotic effusions of Baltimore's citizens; now, instead of remembrance of America's founding, innumerable shoppers are portrayed lined up outside the store awaiting its grand opening. The consumer replaces the citizen; novelty replaces memory.

Gabriel and Izzy also choose to leave the urban community in which they were raised, mimicking that choice made by their parents when they

8   Alan Ehrenhalt, *The Lost City: Discovering the Forgotten Virtues of Community in the Chicago of the 1950's* (New York: Basic Books, 1995), 23.

journeyed to the new world in search of freedom. When told they will be leaving Baltimore for the "suburbs," Michael asks his mother, "What does it mean, the suburbs?" She replies, "It's a nicer place to live—it's got lawns and big trees." Yet, despite this description of the *external* qualities of the suburbs, life there comes to center inside, rather than outside, the home. In Baltimore, daily life is depicted as unfolding largely outside, on the stoops and on the streets of the neighborhood. The discomfort of row-house living is not ignored, particularly during the summer months when both the absence of air-conditioning and the enclosure on two sides by other houses could make interior life stifling and unbearable. Yet, solutions to the absence of air-conditioning are also in evidence: one July 4th, Sam takes Michael and other children to a local lake where they watch fireworks, and then, along with many other families in the neighborhood, remain on the shore to sleep for the night. Sam tells the children stories, and also imparts the ancient wisdom of outdoor sleeping during the summer: "with the breeze, you can sleep." As Sam falls asleep with the children, the camera pans back to reveal hundreds of temporary campers by the water, reposed securely together as they seek the breeze. The scene of a sleeping neighborhood ably captures that lost world of public life described by Ehrenhalt, when people "considered the streets to be their home, an extension of their property, whereas today the streets are, for many people, an alien place. A block is not really a community in this neighborhood anymore. Only a house is a community, a tiny outpost dependent on television and air-conditioning, and accessible to other such outposts, even the nearest ones, almost exclusively by automobile."[9]

As Ehrenhalt's comments would suggest, the film, also about a "lost city," comes increasingly to feature the automobile and the television. With the move to the suburbs, it becomes essential for each of the adult family members to drive in order to reach other family members or to purchase the essentials of life, in contrast to the Baltimore neighborhood which they left, where it is shown that a large open-air market is swarmed by people making their daily purchases, all walking and mingling informally. Eva regards Ann's driving skills with suspicion, but the

9   Ehrenhalt, 255.

film implicitly shows that Ann *must* learn to drive if she is to run a household in the suburbs, even as Eva must increasingly come to rely upon others for transportation.[10] While the move to the suburbs from the city involved an act of definite *choice*, ironically it also removes the choice of whether to learn to drive or not, or whether one increasingly depends on the automobile for one's daily life. One choice leads to the removal of other choices, but that removal is obfuscated by a growing consumer culture that offers myriad choices about brands, models, and makes of automobiles even as people grow unaware that they have the lost the choice whether to own and operate an automobile in the first place.[11]

Television becomes the other star of the film. Upon moving to the suburbs, the family's life comes to center around the television for leisure and even the place where life unfolds, in contrast to the streets and stoops of Baltimore where one retreated in the evening. The family begins to eat its meals in front of the television, or even abandon their meal when the "Milton Berle Show" comes on, eventually opting to put a television in nearly every room, including the kitchen and the bedroom. Toward the film's close, in stark contrast to the film's opening scene of a chaotic

10   Eva believes her suspicions are justified when a street car jumps its tracks and destroys Ann's car. Ironically, while the film explicitly portrays a moment when a public transportation vehicle destroys a privately owned automobile, the true tendency proved to be the opposite—the popularity of automobiles would eventually lead to the dismantling of many systems of urban and suburban public transportation. This dynamic is delightfully explored in the live action/animated film, *Who Framed Roger Rabbit?*

11   As Benjamin R. Barber writes, "the American's freedom to choose among scores of automobile brands was secured by sacrificing the liberty to choose between private and public transportation, and mandated a world in which strip malls, suburbs, high gas consumption, and traffic jams (to name just a few) became inevitable and omnipresent without ever having been the willed choice of some democratic decision making body—or for that matter the individuals who liked driving automobiles and chose to buy one. This politics of commodity . . . offers the feel of freedom while diminishing the range of options and the power to affect the larger world. Is this really liberty?" *Jihad vs. McWorld* (New York: Random House, 1995), 220–01.

but lively Thanksgiving holiday, Gabriel and Ann Kaye eat their Thanksgiving dinners silently seated on the living room couch with their two children, each facing the television as they shovel food into their mouths without remark. While perhaps an overstated example of contemporary American trends, Levinson rightly reminds us the extent to which television has come to be associated with a central familial holiday like Thanksgiving, with entire families often gathering after dinner to watch specially scheduled football games or popular movies.

By the end of the film, television comes to dominate the domestic landscape, and aptly serves as a symbol of the innumerable choices that allowed for the dissipation of the cohesive urban community and added to the isolation of suburban life. Television has come increasingly to mirror and accommodate itself to a lifestyle dominated by a central desire for endless choice, the avoidance of long-term commitments, and an unwillingness to remain in settings that could prove demanding if ultimately rewarding. Ehrenhalt finds television to be a perfect symbol for this culminating obsession with choice over stability:

> Channel surfing is not exactly a metaphor for life, but it isn't a bad caricature of the larger predicaments for the 1990s . . . . Too many of the things we do in our lives, large and small, have come to resemble channel surfing, marked by a numbing and seemingly endless progression from one option to the next, all without the benefit of a chart, logistical or moral, because there are simply too many choices and no one to help sort them out. We have nothing to insulate ourselves against the perpetual temptation to try one more choice, rather than live with what is on the screen in front of us.[12]

Television obscures certain forms of memory even as it imparts new memories. As Sam insisted, "if you stop remembering, you forget"; however, Levinson implies in addition, when one loses the capacity to speak and listen there are no memories to recall. *Avalon's* last scene portrays an adult Michael visiting his grandfather Sam in a nursing home with

12   Ehrenhalt, 271–72.

his son, also named Sam. Michael has grown up in a world of extended families that are not yet completely dissipated, before the dominance of television, steeped in Sam's stories related at countless Thanksgivings and in the semi-public places of pre-suburban life. Young Sam, however, grows up in a world where those institutions have increasingly ceased to exist in the wake of the successful escape of families away from both the encroachments and the richness of urban life. The movie ends as it begins—Sam tells of the day he arrived in America, July 4, 1914—but instead of the attentions of younger generation trained in listening and using their imaginative resources to paint an inner picture based on another's words and stories, young Sam's attention wanders quickly to the television, where the flickering images supplant the need to listen, where words cease to guide and vision is divorced from meaning and memory.[13]

Sam relates that he tried to find Avalon, the name of the apartment house in which he lived with his brothers when he first emigrated to America. America, however, has moved on, uprooting the old to be replaced by the new, obliterating memory in the pursuit of the novel and stylish. Avalon is gone, and Sam's fruitless search to find the physical evidence of his lost past leads Sam to admit that "for a minute, I thought I never was." Close to death, silently wondering about the continuities of existence, Sam recognizes that obscurity and amnesia about the past is the result of a culture of escape.[14] If George Bailey literally plows over the graves of the dead to erect his subdivision, "Avalon" suggests that

13 On the way that visual media obliterates context and memory, see Neil Postman, *Amusing Ourselves to Death: Public Discourse in the Age of Show Business* (New York: Penguin Books, 1985), esp. 99–113.

14 Hannah Arendt describes cohesive political communities as a form of "organized remembrance" in *The Human Condition* (New York: Doubleday & Company, 1959), 176. Such a city "assures the mortal actor that his passing existence and fleeting greatness will never lack the reality that comes from being seen, being heard, and generally appearing before an audience of fellow men . . ." (176–77). See also my discussion on the connection between the embrace of limits, human community, and the possibility of memorial for even the most obscure of humanity in *The Odyssey of Political Theory: The Politics of Departure and Return* (Lanham, MD: Rowman & Littlefied Publishers, 2000), ch. 5.

the move from the "lost city" to the suburban idyll echoes this burying of the past, if not as swiftly and obviously as the bulldozer, nevertheless, over the long term and with help of the automobile and the television, just as thoroughly.

American Beauty: End of Escape?

American Beauty portrays a world in which Bailey Park is ascendant and where the fancy of Ann Kaye to have her "own place" in the suburbs is achieved. Yet, in this film one finds none of the progressive hopes for the future as in *It's a Wonderful Life*. The suburbs are a trap, not an escape, a place where life has become predictable, stale and absent a kind of wonder or enchantment. However, the film also contains none of the nostalgia of *Avalon* for a better place in the distant past, before the exodus from the vibrancy of the cities and the move into an unstable present peopled by strangers. There is no fantasy of escape to a particular *place*, whether from the small town or countryside to the city or suburbs. Yet escape remains as fond a dream as ever, even if it is no longer evident to where one can escape, if escape remains even possible.

"American Beauty" centers on the life of Lester Burnham (Kevin Spacey), a suburban husband who longs to escape the deadening existence of modern American conformity. The film opens with a long shot above an unnamed town, one more affluent than Bailey Park but composed of houses built along a similar design, if larger and more comfortable. As the camera zooms in to reveal a tidy suburban street lined with trees and neat houses, Lester intones in a voiceover: "This is my neighborhood. This is my street. This is my life." He then tells us, "In less than a year I'll be dead. In a way, I'm dead already." The film centers on the brief period of time between Lester's observation of his existence as a "living dead" until his actual death, and describes how he comes to embrace life even as death approaches.

Lester's existence is portrayed as sterile, predictable, and wholly uninteresting. He detests his job, and his family appears to detest him. The sterile neighborhood represents nearly the full extent of life for the Burnham family, aside from stultifying work, clique-driven school, and a dissatisfying family life inside the home. In the neighborhood, there is a gay professional couple named Jim and Jim, and a new family that moves into the house next-door to the Burnhams. Like the Burnhams, these new neighbors are a small nuclear family, comprised of a father— Colonel Frank Fitts—a mother who appears to be autistic, and a son, Ricky Fitts (Wes Bentley). Colonel Fitts is a homophobic autocrat who collects Nazi paraphernalia, tests his son's urine for drugs, and beats Ricky when he disobeys. Ricky, in turn, puts on an act of abject obedience for his father, but in fact sells drugs throughout the town.

That which is usually shown to be "normal" in most American television shows and movies—the suburban nuclear family—is portrayed in "American Beauty" as a repository of deceit, conformity, materialism, marital—and especially sexual—discontent, selfishness, anxiety, psychological disorder, substance abuse, even outright violence and hysteria. Indeed, the only "well-adjusted" and traditionally "normal" family that appears during the course of the film is the gay couple, Jim and Jim, who appear at the Fitts's door with a generous house-warming gift, and maintain informal neighborly contact with the Burnhams.

Lester is suddenly awoken from his conformist slumber one evening while attending a basketball game. There, watching his daughter's friend Angela perform a cheerleading routine, Lester becomes nearly obsessed with the promise of youth. Into his disenchanted world explodes a fantasy of color, texture, sight and sound, represented by deep red rose petals that continue to appear in any fantasy involving Angela. Later that evening, envisioning Angela surrounded by rose petals, we hear him realize that he's been in "a coma . . . for twenty years, and I'm only now waking up."

In the theme of "sleeping" and "awakening" one hears echoes of that classic American tract of non-conformity, Henry David Thoreau's *Walden*. As Thoreau describes, one must will wakefulness against the temptations of conformist sleep: "We must learn to reawaken and keep ourselves awake, not by mechanical aids, but by an infinite expectation of the dawn, which does not forsake us in our soundest sleep."[15] Almost as if describing Lester before his epiphany induced by the cheerleaders,

15 Henry David Thoreau, *Walden and Other Writings* (New York: Random House, 1965), 81.

Thoreau writes that "by closing the eyes and slumbering, and consenting to be deceived by shows, men establish and confirm their daily life of routine and habit everywhere, which still is built on purely illusory foundations. Children, who play life, discern its true law and relations more clearly than men, who fail to live it worthily, but who think that they are wiser by experience, that is, by failure."[16] As Lester rebels from this unreal life he leads, he adopts ever more the perspective of a child, attempting to recapture his own youth by reliving various experiences of his adolescence. He quits his job by means of his rebellious "job description" for management; he begins smoking marijuana supplied by Ricky; at Angela's suggestive prompting, he begins lifting weights, and eventually sets up a combination weight room/drug den in his garage. He takes a job at a "Smiley Burger" franchise where he works at the drive-through window. He seeks to relive the freedom of his youth, a time when "all I did was party and get laid. I had my whole life ahead of me . . . ."

Lester seems to follow the teachings of Henry Thoreau in *Walden* through his rejection of civilization's expectations and his disdain for materialism. Yet, Lester's rebellion seems in many respects a pale shadow, even a laughable parody of Thoreau's move away from civilization. If there is any "place" that resembles the retreat that Thoreau's Walden Pond represents, it is Lester's garage. Hardly a repose of natural solitude, his garage—that architectural feature that gained prominence at the time of developments such as Bailey Park—is a place that is both *not* his home, therefore representing a place *apart*, yet still attached to his home, still within the bounds of what is safe, predictable—apparently non-conformist even as his mortgage covers the costs.

Similarly, although Lester quits his job in an act of apparent bold confrontation with the inanities of management, he succeeds in extorting a full year's pay and benefits from his immediate boss when he threatens him with false charges of sexual harassment. His rebellion will be financed by corporate America, including his health and retirement benefits. One detail of Lester's town we discover later is that he lives on Robin Hood Trail, a telling irony since he steals from the rich in order to give to himself, one who is hardly poor but wishes to

16 Thoreau, 86.

pretend to disregard material possessions without the discomforts that poverty would entail. In a late scene in which he tries to seduce Carolyn by reminding her of how vivacious and fun she was as a younger woman, she breaks the spell by warning him that he is about to spill beer on the living room sofa. Infuriated at this petty observation, Lester explodes at her: "So what, it's just a couch. This isn't life. It's just *stuff*. It's become more important to you than living." One marvels at Lester's accusation of Carolyn's materialism here, for the scene began with Lester declaring to Carolyn that he has just purchased a 1970 Pontiac Firebird, "the car I've always wanted. And now I have it. I rule." Lester's rebellion is financed by corporate America, comprised of adolescent retreat into the garage (where, for generations, teenagers have gone to practice in their makeshift bands) and prurient fantasies about underaged girls, and symbolized by the purchase of youthful muscle-cars.

Lester is ultimately awoken from his "awakening" when he finally has the opportunity for a sexual liason with Angela. As he disrobes her, he discovers—notwithstanding her braggadocio—she is what she appears to be, a vulnerable, sexually inexperienced girl. Lester suddenly "awakens"—again—and appears to recognize the shallowness of his "rebellion." As he contemplates a picture of his family, in which each member smiles unassumingly at some point in the obscured past, Lester is shot from behind by Colonel Fitts, a man contorted by his own homoerotic longings that Lester has rejected. In the moments before death, Lester engages in a nostalgia for a purer past, a past that symbolized the true happiness of his life—picturing himself as a Boy Scout, his grandmother's hands, his cousin's Firebird, Jane as a girl, and Carolyn as a young woman. One can only relive the past through memory, not through the literal attempt to recapture an adolescent past as an adult.

Achieving a kind of clarity at the moment of death, Lester imparts to us the wisdom of that moment. As his soul rises above the town, his voiceover intones:

> I guess I could be pretty pissed about what happened to me, but it's hard to stay mad when there's so much beauty in the world. Then I remember to relax, and stop trying to hold onto

it. Then it flows through me like rain. I can't feel anything but gratitude for every single moment of my stupid little life. You have no idea what I'm talking about I'm sure. But don't worry—you will, someday.

Lester's soul flies above the city into the clouds, and we have a final image of the only form of actual escape in an age when all other avenues are closed—the gratitude for a lived life that comes at death. It is knowledge that we can't have now—we have "no idea" what Lester is talking about—but will come someday, since death comes to us all.

However, one wonders if Lester has in fact gained a special kind of wisdom at the film's end, whether death has given him some special insight into human happiness. For, in keeping with that oldest feature of the American character, it is only through escape—literally pictured as he ascends above and away from his town—that Lester realizes the abiding value of the events of his now-passed life. In a revelation comparable to that of George Bailey, Lester understands that he led "a wonderful life," but one that gains credence in retrospect, not as it's lived. The disdain for the conformity and sterility of late twentieth-century American suburban life is not dismissed, only obscured by the distance that the camera provides as it pans outward and away. The film finally does not pose any suggestions or potential remedies for the anomic life of the nuclear American family, seemingly trapped in the place to which so many for so long sought escape. In contrast to the other films under examination, there is no evidence of an extended family in "American Beauty," no network of familial bonds or friendships built over time in an intimate and stable community. Lester's apparently profound concluding remarks are in fact revealed to be wholly facile when one considers the film's concluding recommendation for how to live in a setting that it so obviously disdains. Cynicism until the moment of the death is the order of the day, when redemption will be provided at the moment of final escape. The frontier is closed; return to Eden is forestalled; community is quaint, impossible, and finally too limiting. Political remedies are non-existent, as politics is as entirely absent as grandparents or trusted neighbors. All that remains is the hope of escape in the future and the willful disdain of our American present now. Awakening from our American dream of escape, we discover that it was a nightmare all along, a fond wish that brought us to the point of hating what we so desperately craved, of despising what we have become, and of no longer seeing how we can find a way toward escape from the interminable vision of escape.

Part 2
Thinking Conservatively

Chapter 5

Manners and Morals: Or, Why You Should Not Eat the Person Sitting Next to You

Several years ago I was invited to deliver a lecture to a group of young, bright college students on the subject of "Manners and Morals." The subject was all that was assigned; it was up to me to define the specific content and theme of the lecture. For several days I approached with trepidation the blank document with the title at its head, "Manners and Morals," and beat a quick retreat each time, with growing trepidation that I was not equal to the task of imagination.

As I mulled over my predicament after several days lacking inspiration or direction, my head hung low and on the verge of tears, my then 9-year-old son came up behind me and, glancing over my shoulder, saw that I was to be speaking on "Manners and Morals." And I can only attribute what happened next to some kind of divine intervention, because he looked at me with all earnestness and said, "Oh, I guess you'll be telling the students why they should eat with forks." I looked at him, and, a smile growing on my face, said, "Yes, that's exactly right." "Because that's being a civilized person?" he asked. "Yes, that's why." My son clearly saw what had been eluding me: it was the fork that made the connections between manners, morals, and civilization and finally the highest aspirations of religion self-evident. So, at the risk of belaboring what must now be equally obvious to my reader, I will expound about Manners, Morals, and Religion, alternatively wearing the hats of an amateur anthropologist, a professional political theorist, and a wholly inadequate theologian. It may seem a lot to undertake, but it's nothing that Miss Manners doesn't do every day.

I think we can all agree that of all the problems facing humanity, from war to poverty, from the threats emanating from human technology and progress to the possibility of killer asteroids, perhaps the most pressing and challenging problem we all face is teaching kids how to eat. Let's face it: they're like wild beasts, and if they could run around naked eating with their hands, dropping half their food behind them and going back later when they're hungry again to eat off the ground what's left, they would. Anyone who has an idyllic fantasy of peaceful and heart-warming family dinners in which conversation flows freely and gentle wit punctuates gradually unfolding dinner courses hasn't been over to my house for dinner recently. Dinner is a kind of near state of barely restrained anarchy. "Use your fork." "Don't lick your plate." "Stop putting your knife in your mouth." "Sit up." "Sit back down." "Don't mash your peas." "No, you can't eat that piece from your brother's plate (or, alternatively, no, you can't put your food on his plate)." "Don't talk with your mouth full." "You forgot to ask to be excused." On and on and on. Incredibly, all one seems to do as a parent is to repeat the same things over and over and over. Kids hate it, and parents get frustrated. Why do we bother? What's the point of good manners?

The easy answer is, so that someday we can have peaceful and heart-warming family dinners in which conversation flows freely and gentle wit punctuates gradually unfolding dinner courses. Teaching manners is to instill a second nature to a child, to habituate: to eat with grace is not natural to them, but someday we hope it will become "second nature" for them to eat with a fork and knife, not to take food from other people's plates, and to excuse themselves when they leave the table. I compare it to my experience coaching my son's Little League baseball team when they were very young. Day after day, week after week, we did drills—when to throw to first, who covers second, where the cutoff man stands, how to execute a rundown. At first, it's incredibly painful—the height of unnaturalness for children, and for a long time they're uncertain what they should be doing. Then, eventually, they start to make some plays, some of the drills click, and you can begin to see some inkling of the beauty of the game when well-played. That year when my son was nine years old, our team had a 1-12 record in the regular season, but we had a Bad News Bears run through the playoffs, and came home with the championship. Knowing where to move on the field had become second nature, but only through a very lengthy process of cultivation and habituation. That's the aim with table manners as well, painful as it may be to get to there.

As I say, that's the easy answer. It addresses a superficial why, but not the deeper reasons. Why do parents (some, though certainly not enough) exert so much energy in cultivating manners in their children? Are they sinister instruments of torture, as my children believe? What purpose do they serve? Do children know? Do parents know?

As ever, we turn to Aristotle for the answer. In the *Politics*, Aristotle writes: "For just as man, when he is perfected (when he achieves his *telos*) is the best of animals, so too separated from law and justice he is the worst of all . . . . Without virtue he is most unholy and savage, and worst in regards to sex and eating." Aristotle doesn't spell out what he means by this last comment, but it's pretty clear that humans who lack virtue—who live without law and justice—exhibit the worst forms of human behavior in matters of sex and eating, engaging in what remain, even in our own incredibly permissive time, two largely acknowledged taboos—incest and cannibalism.

Aristotle is not saying that children or humans generally have to be taught how to eat or how to copulate. That's something we all pretty much figure out on our own at some point—instinct kicks in as a baby in the case of eating, and in the case of sex, well, that will come in good time. Both these instincts are deeply embedded in our nature—we *must* eat to continue living, we must copulate in order to reproduce.

But that's about all that nature tells us in these matters: eat to live; copulate to procreate. That's all that nature needs to tell to all God's creatures—all, that is, except mankind. Nature's admonition to eat and to procreate is not the whole of the story, in our case, because we are creatures not solely in the thrall of nature. *Natural* features of humanity cause us to act according to our natures with a degree of reflection and choice. As Leon Kass has argued in his marvelous book, *The Hungry Soul*, the human form itself resists our "mere" nature.[1] Our upright

---

1   Leon R. Kass, M.D., *The Hungry Soul* (Chicago: University of Chicago Press, 1999). The whole of this essay is greatly influenced by Kass's magnificent study of food and ethics. At best this piece is an effort to extend his insights into the realm of politics.

form places us above the horizon, making it possible to see further visually and metaphorically gives us the ability to set our sights to higher things. Our mouth and nose—set down and back in the skulls, unlike the snout of other beasts—means that our eyes purposively lead and guide our eating faculties, not vice-versa. Our tongues and lips, in addition to assisting in the process of eating, also have a form which permits the faculty of speech and communication. Our omnivorousness gives us actual and metaphorical preferences; we pick and choose what we will eat, given the opportunity, just as we exercise choice about how we will eat, and even further, how we will live. We are conscious and self-reflective; we are conscious too of the preferences of others by dint of the fact of speech and reason. It is thus in our nature not only to eat and to copulate, but to ask about the meaning of these things and to ask whether there are better and worse ways to engage in these natural necessities and urges.[2] As Erwin Straus has written, "Considering [man's form], we do well to envisage the possibility that [it is] not society [which] has first brought man into conflict with nature, but that [it is] man's natural opposition to nature [which] enables him to produce society, history, and conventions."[3] This Aristotelian insight suggests, contra Rousseau, that it is in our nature to be "unnatural." Better put, humanity can act in accordance with nature most humanly as a result of a training in virtue, or alternatively, can act in accordance with nature *least* humanly when we act blindly in the thrall of those basest instincts as a brute or beast. To fulfill man's natural telos is to act in ways *not* most immediately "natural." We might say that man is by nature a conventional animal.

The simple reason that humans have the potential to be unholy and savage in matters of eating is because, as omnivores, we are inclined to eat meat. This means that we are a predatory animal: one of our most primal desires impels us to kill. To kill is an awesome deed: our desire to sustain our lives drives us to combat and overcome the survival instinct of other living creatures. In this, we are primally no different

2   Kass, *The Hungry Soul*, ch. 2.
3   Erwin Straus, "The Upright Posture," in *Phenomenological Psychology* (New York: Basic Books, 1986), 142.

than the lion or the wolf: we must kill other animals in order to slake our craving for meat. Indeed, we are the most successful predatory animal that has ever existed on earth—no animal can for long protect itself from us when we decide upon its death. Our diet reveals our rapacity, our potential for savagery, the very "inhumanity" of our humanity.

The fact that we eat meat also means that we can eat each other. This is not unknown in nature, and of course is not unknown among some human civilizations. The Aztecs ritually sacrificed and ate hundreds of thousands of captives, removing first their still beating hearts as a sacrifice to their sun god and then devouring the remains. Cannibalism is not literally unthinkable, though I much doubt many of us think about it very much if at all—and that's a good thing too. As W. H. Auden wrote in his *A Commonplace Book*, "The slogan of Hell: Eat or be eaten."[4] To live among people who were always sizing you up as a meal—and perhaps even worse, in which you were doing the same—would be a living hell, worse than Hobbes's State of Nature. There could be no stability, no decency, no trust, no love.

Society as we know it could not exist if we weighed cannibalism as a serious option for our diet. The fact that we do not weigh and consider, much less *think* about cannibalism, is a silent reminder of civilized humanity's longstanding virtuous decision in which we have concluded that human beings are not food. The negative formulation—humans are not food—implicitly reveals a positive formulation: that human beings are creatures set apart because of their inherent dignity and nobility. It is the very decision not to eat humans that fundamentally reveals the truth of our dignity: we are uniquely the creature that commands itself, that exercises restraint over appetite and instinct and discriminates between human and non-human (sometimes that gets us into trouble, but it is fundamentally a praiseworthy faculty). Man is by nature the ethical animal: all ethics begins in injunctions, in saying *No*, and the most primal ethical decision concerns what we will eat and what will not be eaten.

4   W. H. Auden, *A Certain World: A Commonplace Book* (New York: Viking, 1970), 134.

Nevertheless, in the deepest recesses of our collective memory and in the most primal depths of our hearts, we know that to eat meat is dangerous and awe-inspiring. Table manners are the inscribed tradition—practice and custom—that reflects and in some senses commemorates this conscious decision to ascend from brute appetite and to demonstrate that we are not slaves to our cravings. Next time you sit down with an anti-traditionalist, see if they eat by tearing their food apart with their hands, or by eating with their faces in their plates. We are all traditionalists, and it's a good thing too.

Even as we employ our manners as we eat—for we MUST eat—manners demonstrate that we seek to constrain and moderate, if not fully to extinguish, our natures. Manners are conventions that shape and govern our nature: we don't cease to be creatures that must eat, but manners are a largely unconscious demonstration of our governance of our nature as eating creatures, even as we necessarily submit to and even engage in a more exalted practice of our nature. Far from being a troublesome and meaningless set of conventions, table manners are the daily manifestation of our commitment to the aspiration of human flourishing, of a realized humanity that ascends from "mere" or given humanity. To be a human is to be conventional, and among those most important conventions that express our humanity is to mediate, moderate, and master our appetites through the conventions at dinner time.

Consider for a moment the humble fork. If you have one nearby, put down this book for a moment and pick it up. Feel it, weigh it, look at its form and shape. Now, daily we admire and marvel at various technologies, from the nifty features on IPODS to the cameras that are phones, or phones that are cameras, and so on. But, how often in recent days, weeks, or years, have you admired a fork? This is a signal piece of human technology that we take for granted, usually three times a day every day. We are likely altogether unaware of forks—we use them unselfconsciously—as their use has become our "second nature." The only time we are likely to think about utensils is when we go out to Chinese or Japanese or Ethiopian restaurants. Our very unconsciousness hides their considerable achievement from us.

Our knowledge of forks dates back to the eleventh century, although they don't become widespread for another five centuries and not universal in the West until the nineteenth century.[5] The longstanding manner of using utensils before the introduction of the fork was to eat using one's knife. In fact, as people in Europe moved away from eating with their hands, they began eating with two knives—one to cut and deliver the food to the mouth, the other to hold down the piece of meat. However, as anyone who has ever used this method knows, inevitably the piece of meat starts to turn around in circle on the axis of the second knife. The first use of the fork was as a two-pronged instrument that could hold down the meat (and still takes the same form as a carving fork), after which the pieces were still brought to the mouth balanced upon the knife.

The development of four tines was a long time coming—first people used the version of a carving fork to eat, but that was highly impracticable. Eventually, the formation of the fork anticipated the development of the Gillette razor blade—if two tines was good, why not more and more and more? Anything over six tines forced eaters to open their mouths in a wholly unseemly fashion, and five tines reminded people too much of the fingers on our hands—which the fork was designed explicitly to replace—so the appropriate number of tines was settled upon to be four. It is not arbitrary: it is a convention guided by our natures as eaters, as meat-eaters, as five-fingered, as creatures with mouths of a certain width. The fork is the height of human engineering.

The fork does not make eating food easier—it makes it more difficult. By using the fork, we bring food in small portions to our mouths. As my son knows, it's much faster to eat either by putting your face in your plate or just using your fingers. We have a particular challenge with rice—it's hard to eat rice with a fork, so he tries endlessly to position his mouth next to his plate and use his fork as a bulldozer. We end up having to sweep a lot of rice off the floor as a consequence of our insistence that he eat by raising his food to his mouth. What this allows, of course, in addition to a slowing of the pace of the eating, is the posture of face-to-face dinners. We eat in such a way that makes it possible for us to see one another (even as part of good manners is not to look

---

5   For much of the following discussion of the history of utensils, I am grateful to Margaret Visser's wonderful book *The Rituals of Dinner* (New York: Penguin, 1992).

too closely at another person eating), and more importantly, to speak with one another as we eat. By eating with forks—with utensils generally—we raise our heads above our food and communicate. We forge community.

The fork was introduced because over time it became unacceptable to use the knife except when absolutely necessary. The knife is a visible sign of the violence that underlies our meals, and civilization eventually sought to minimize its use, and even when it was used, to make its function nearly unrecognizable. Notice some features of the kind of knife that we typically use at a typical meal. The end of the standard knife is rounded, not pointed, and it's somewhat difficult to cut much of anything with the barely sharpened blade. Note that in fine restaurants when you order steak, a knife is brought to you from the kitchen only when the meat is served, and cleared as soon as the meal is finished. As we eat using fork and knife, various customs encourage a certain infelicity and awkwardness. In Europe, the knife is held in the weaker hand, making it less likely there will be knife play at the table. In America, food is cut with the knife in the right hand and the fork in the left; after each cut, the utensils are switched to the opposite hand and that single piece is eaten. Americans are regularly subjected to scorn and derision for this awkward practice. However, let me quote from the Harvard Olin lecture of Judith Martin, a.k.a. Miss Manners, who defends such a practice: "American table manners are, if anything, a more advanced form of civilized behavior than the European, because they are more complicated and further removed from the practical result, always a sign of refinement."[6]

Table manners contain and reflect the governance of our basest nature—that we will eat deliberately, in a measured fashion, with layers of convention and practice that partially obscures our potential for bestiality. Manners, we might say, are the visible sign of our depravity, our inclination to submit to appetite. Manners are a constant reminder of our fallen nature: as Byron wrote, "ever since Eve ate apples, much depends on dinner." Original sin is inextricably bound up with the human inability

6   Judith Martin, *Common Courtesy: In Which Miss Manners Solves the Problem that Baffled Mr. Jefferson* (New York: Scribner, 1985).

to control our appetite; manners are the form that forces a degree of control upon us. Manners are a form of what Aristotle calls "habituation": they are practices ingrained into us when we are young and not yet wholly conscious of their meaning, necessary foundations for the virtuous human who would act with moderation and prudence, *sophrosune* and *phronesis*. At the same time, manners point also to our higher nature. To have manners, as my son knows but perhaps does not yet fully understand, is to be civilized. Manners aspire to civility.

One of the better articulations of manners occurs in one of the best, and one of the most deeply conservative movies in recent years, "Blast From the Past." In the film, a young man is raised in a bomb shelter for several decades after his father has falsely believed that the "big one" was dropped on Los Angeles. While the culture decays above ground, "Adam" is raised in accordance with the cultural norms that prevailed in the 1950s. Upon his twenty-fifth birthday he ascends to the upper world to accumulate new supplies and the comedy of manners begins.

During his encounter with what he comes to believe to be the "mutants" who have survived in the aftermath of the nuclear holocaust, he encounters a young woman (named "Eve," of course) and her gay friend "Troy." They are the very studies of modern-day world-weariness, irony and skepticism, and wonder at the creature they have encountered whose earnestness, courteousness and decency they cannot comprehend. In one significant conversation, Eve and Troy have the following exchange about Adam's good manners.

Troy: "He said that good manners are a way of showing people that we have respect for them. I didn't know that. I thought it was a way of acting all superior."

Eve: "Where do you think he got all that information?"

Troy: "From the oddest place—his parents."

We practice manners in the main in order to put others at ease—they are, to a significant extent, outer-directed. Ironically, manners are an acknowledgement that we are not given to care about each other. Respect is different from care. As the sociologist Edward Shils has written in his book entitled *Civility*, "There is not enough good nature or temperamental amiability in any society to permit to it to dispense with good man-

ners."[7] But, such habituation in manners—a sign of our permanent di-
videdness and insufficient stores of unquestioning love for every human
being—at the same time also points to our potential for flourishing communal life. To eat with manners is to slow down our food intake, to force
us to face one another as we slowly dine. We make time in order to speak
and to listen. By holding at bay our primal instinct to gorge ourselves as
quickly and efficiently as possible—by restraining our self-interest and
practicing self-governance—we foster opportunities for human inter-
change which may simply remain "civil," but which may also lead to
friendship and even love. By governing the low, we make possible the
high.

Civility and politeness, not surprisingly, relate to public things: each
word means, at base, "city"—"cives" in Latin, *polis* in Greek. While
table manners seems like a wholly private affair—something taught by
one's parents for use at one's private meals—manners inevitably involves
and aspires to a public dimension. We know from the Odyssey that the
Cyclops did not have good table manners. Indeed, he was a cannibal—
he snatches up pairs of Odysseus's men, beats their brains out on the
cave wall, and eats them raw. We also know the following from the
poet—lines that Aristotle also quotes in the *Politics*:

> we sailed further
> along, and reached the country of the lawless outrageous
> Cyclopes who, putting all their trust in the immortal
> gods, neither plow with their hands nor plant anything,
> but all grows for them without seed planting, without cultivation.
> These people have no institutions, no meetings for councils;
> rather they make their habitations in caverns hollowed
> among the peaks of high mountains, and each one is the law
> for his own wives and children, and cares nothing about the others.[8]

---

7   Edward Shils, *The Virtue of Civility: Selected Essays on Liberalism, Tradition and Civil Society.* Edited by Steven Grosby (Indianapolis, IN: Liberty
Fund, 1997).

8   Homer, *The Odyssey*, translated by Richmond Lattimore (New York:
HarperCollins, 1965), 9, 105–15.

Cyclops has one eye—he is more bestial than human, more directed by his appetite than by his vision. Because the Cyclopes have no community, they have no culture (literally, they do not cultivate)—no rituals, no arts or *techne*, no *memory*. When Polyphemus is blinded by Odysseus, the joke is really on his fellow Cyclopes, who are more inclined to believe that "Noman" injured him than to be concerned about his bellows of pain. Because Cyclopes cannot distinguish between man and beast—indeed, Polyphemus is quite solicitous toward his sheep—they are creatures without ethics and politics; they lack the guiding conventions that result from the self-governance that itself arises from the recognition of human distinctiveness and dignity.

Impolite people are likely to be without politics; people without a city are unlikely to be civil. There is not a strict private/public divide here: that which inclines humans to adopt manners also inclines those humans to foster community with their companions and hospitality toward strangers. To eat together is to seek out others for reasons that go beyond mere utility, to seek companionship—literally, a word whose Latin root means literally "to break bread with." A really brief description of what happens in the *Odyssey* is eat first, ask questions later. To eat together is to converse; to converse is to make the primary human interaction one of shared speech rather than threatened or real violence. Indeed, *conversari* is a Latin word meaning "to turn oneself about" or "to move to and fro." Conversation implies a willingness to move oneself, metaphorically, to leave oneself in considering the views of another, even to be persuaded (again, here words are revealing: in the Greek, the passive of "to persuade" [*peitho*] is not strictly "to be persuaded," but "to trust"). Civility and politeness imply politics and life in the city.

Aristotle writes that "man is by nature a political animal." Man is by nature the creature that must live according to convention—under law, with self-restraint against nature's imperatives, by means of a flourishing that can only come about as the result of habituation, education, cultivation. He who is without a city is either a beast or a god. The human telos can only come to fruition within cities of humans: leisure, arts, learning, memory, culture, philosophy, even worship—these are activities that rely fundamentally upon the existence of human cities. Politics begins with politeness—with good manners. Rather than figuratively or literally eating up our opponents, we must dine with them. As T. S. Eliot wrote, "the survival of a parliamentary system requires constant dining with opponents." Politics, like manners, is the visible manifestation of our willingness to restrain ourselves and to govern our immediate appetites in order to live and even thrive together. The city is like a fork. It is a contrived invention intended to slow us down, to "ruminate," to put some psychic distance from our immediate whim and to give us time to "converse," to turn ourselves about. Politics cannot be run on an economic or philosophic ideological model: it cannot be based upon pure interest nor can it wholly transcend interest. Like eating, we can control and restrain how we eat, but we must eat – politics must be driven by interest, even if it is interest and appetite moderated and transformed. Politics does not transcend nature—again, like the four-tined fork, it is the invention appropriate to our nature (though humans have long debated which regime—how many people, like how many tines—ought to govern). If it's harder to know exactly the form a regime should take, like the fork, it should not be too big nor too small: it should permit us only small portions and not allow us to open our mouths too wide. It should slow us down enough to speak, but not so much that we starve. Politics needs to find the mean between extremes of nature and convention.

We don't debate that much about regimes anymore—we are all democrats now. In some senses, democracy is the regime that best proves the superiority and necessity of human manners: rather than some elites needing good manners, in a democracy, the entire citizenry needs good manners. That's a good part of the reason why I believe for most of world history most thinkers were opposed to democracy: seeing the table manners of most common people, they concluded that it would not be a good idea to give them the vote. The rise of democracy in modern times has directly corresponded to the universal adoption of the fork. Democracy has been made possible by the triumph of aristocratic manners. When we teach our kids how to eat with a fork and knife, we are educating them to be good citizens. To have good manners is to acknowledge the possibility of the common good. To be civilized is to be a citizen.

But, here we have a problem. Democracy is the regime based upon equality, and it was Alexis de Tocqueville who pointed out with particular force and clarity that democratic equality is impatient with forms.[9] Forms appear to be precious and uppity—they are aristocratic (recall the conversation between Eve and Troy). *Seinfeld* fans will recall the episode in which Elaine sees Mr. Pitt eating a Snickers bar with a fork and knife. Mr. Pitt is an old aristocrat—he even has a British accent, which is the sure sign that he's either a villain or royalty. Elaine mentions this to George, who is quite intrigued by this eating method and adopts it for himself. As the episode goes on, more and more people adopt this eating method, until by the end of the episode Jerry enters the diner—the quintessential American locale—to see that everyone is eating "finger foods" with a fork and knife. It's funny, precisely because we know it's so absurd.

Think instead of the prevailing American portrayal of good manners. Typically, Americans now have the admirable global mission of teaching the world how to act like philistines. In films like *King Ralph*, the *Princess Diaries*, or any untold number of films in this genre, the coarse American is brought to Europe where he or she receives a crash course

9   "Men living in democratic ages do not readily comprehend the utility of forms: they feel an instinctive contempt for them, I have elsewhere shown for what reasons. Forms excite their contempt and often their hatred; as they commonly aspire to none but easy and present gratifications, they rush onwards to the object of their desires, and the slightest delay exasperates them. This same temper, carried with them into political life, renders them hostile to forms, which perpetually retard or arrest them in some of their projects.

"Yet this objection which the men of democracies make to forms is the very thing which renders forms so useful to freedom; for their chief merit is to serve as a barrier between the strong and the weak, the ruler and the people, to retard the one and give the other time to look about him. Forms become more necessary in proportion as the government becomes more active and more powerful, while private persons are becoming more indolent and more feeble. Thus democratic nations naturally stand more in need of forms than other nations, and they naturally respect them less. This deserves most serious attention."

Alexis de Tocqueville, *Democracy in America,* Trans. Henry Reeve (Boston: J. Allyn, 1876), Vol. 2, Part 4, ch. 7.

in good manners. Of course, this proves offensive to our relaxed and informal American sensibility, and we delight in the American Revolution, Take 2. By the end of the film, Americans teach Europeans how to have a good time (in *The Princess Diaries 2*, Julie Andrews—playing the Queen of England—partakes in mattress sledding in the royal palace). Europe just needs to loosen up and relax. We love Julia Roberts because audiences identified with her in *Pretty Woman* when she went out to the fine restaurant and did not know which fork to use. As Miss Manners writes, "The idea that good table manners indicate a lack of humility is still with us; to this day, a great many people brag about not knowing which fork to use . . . . The rationale that etiquette should be eschewed because it fosters inequality does not ring true in a society that openly admits to a feverish interest in the comparative status-conveying qualities of sneakers. — This stands to reason, that Americans emphasize distinctions that are inherently meaningless—since this is the only kind of distinction we can allow ourselves to accept—while rejecting those forms that are imbued with significance."[10]

Think about America's culinary contributions to the world—whether we invented them or not, we have created worldwide markets in hamburgers, hot dogs, pizza, chicken nuggets, ice cream cones, coffee in paper cups with sipping lids and "sleeves" to protect the fingers from burning—and the list can go on and on. What do these foods have in common? First and most importantly, these foods can be eaten or drunk without utensils, without plates or cups that must be washed. They are made to be eaten figuratively, and often literally, on the run. They are a physical manifestation of what Tocqueville described to be an inescapable feature of modern mass democracy: restlessness. Proud of his freedom, democratic man is nevertheless tormented by the openness of democratic society born of the universal "equality of conditions"—a condition that permits the possibility of meteoric ascent but also constantly threatens headlong decline.

Democratic man is denied a resting place, since to rest is to submit to drift, and to drift in a democratic age is tantamount to sinking. In spite of the "well-being" of democratic man, he is *"restless"*: literally, inca-

10   Judith Martin, *Common Courtesy*.

pable of stillness, rest, leisure, therefore resistant to its concomitant goods—association, companionship, community, conversation, and philosophy. Democratic man seeks always to peer around the next corner, fearful something better lies beyond, and thus necessarily discontent with whatever decencies of the street on which he might live. Motion and dynamism is his lot—both a promise, and a curse. Tocqueville writes:

> In the United States, a man carefully builds a dwelling in which to pass his declining years, and he sells it while the roof is being laid; he plants a garden and he rents it out just as he was going to taste its fruits; he clears a field and leaves to others the care of harvesting its crops. He embraces a profession and quits it.[11]

We invented a phrase for the kind of fueling that such a mobile society requires: fast food. We do not dine; we chew and we inhale. We eat everywhere, all the time: the very enslavement to our biological processes—to our instinct to eat on a whim, and to eat anything—is now aggravated by "culture." Rather than culture restraining our instincts, culture now does the opposite of cultivating—it reinforces our animality. Leon Kass has gotten a lot of fire for prudishness and priggishness for a passage in *The Hungry Soul* that expresses his dismay over the eating of ice cream on the street, but consider the whole passage in its context:

> Eating on the street—even when undertaken, say, because one is between appointments and has no other time to eat—displays in fact precisely . . . a lack of self-control. It betokens enslavement to the belly. Hunger must be sated now; it cannot wait. Though the walking street-eater still moves in the direction of his vision, he shows himself as a being led by his appetites. Lacking utensils for cutting and lifting to the mouth, he will often be seen using his teeth for tearing off chewable portions, just as any animal. Eating on the run does not allow the human way of enjoying one's food, for it is more like

11 Tocqueville, *Democracy in America,* Vol. 2, Part 2, ch. 13.

simple fueling; it is hard to savor or even to know what one is eating when the main point is to hurriedly fill the belly, now running on empty.[12]

A civilization that devotes itself to the most efficient and swift forms of "food delivery" must thereby seek to obscure the relationship of food from its sources and the activities that go into the cultivation and preparation of food. Thomas Jefferson believed that democracy could only flourish with a large proportion of its citizens engaged in agriculture. Jefferson believed that such "yeoman farmers" would leaven democratic society as a whole, practicing their craft as small owners and producers while cultivating not only crops, but also necessary accompanying virtues such as frugality, moderation, self-sufficiency, as well as humility and even piety (witnessed by the fact that we can plant, but we do not control the weather).[13]

---

12   Leon Kass, *The Hungry Soul*, 149.
13   As the author Charles Fish has written about his farming forebears,

> For Grandmother and my uncles, there was an imagined coexistence of the hand of God and the workings of nature that was midway between divinity and the operations of mechanical laws. They would have been uncomfortable if pressed to describe the relationship between the two or to declare whether they believed there was none. When weather or disease caused damage, it was nature, not God, that was named, but nature was not simply a malevolent force. While they had to fight her as she sought to dissolve the artful bonds which held things in useful forms, they also felt they were cooperating with her as they made use of her powers of renewal and growth. They would have listened without objection to the phrase "harnessing the power of nature," but it is unlikely that in their hearts they ever thought they could do it except in the most partial way. Through nature they could accomplish fine things, but that nature herself was ever under their control would have struck them as not quite blasphemous but erroneous and perhaps presumptuous. There was much to remind them that they were not the lords of creation . . . . What fell to their hands to do they did with all their strength and craft, but they knew they worked at the center of a mystery, the motions of which they could neither influence nor predict.

But surely, too, it would also follow from Jefferson's beliefs that a virtue that would be increasingly lost as we leave the farms is a kind of *practical knowledge*, now of the very sources of our sustenance—where it comes from, how it is grown and prepared, the fact that a *civilization* is premised upon how it produces and consumes food. A civilization is, most fundamentally, the collective effort to feed ourselves in a predictable and ongoing manner. The "civilization" of fast food seeks entirely to divorce its producers from its consumers, to render our food largely unrecognizable by means of the very convenience of production and conveyability of its form. In the words of the farmer and writer Wendell Berry, a civilization divorced from a deeper knowledge of its sources of sustenance will be suffused in ignorance and deeply prone to abuse.

> Most of us get almost all the things we need by buying them; most of us know only vaguely, if at all, where these things come from; and most of us know not at all what damage is involved in their production. We are almost entirely dependent on an economy of which we are almost entirely ignorant. The provenance, for example, not only of the food we buy at the store, but of the chemicals, fuels, metals, and other materials necessary to grow, harvest, transport, process, and package that food is almost necessarily a mystery to us. To know the full economic history of a head of supermarket cauliflower would require an immense job of research.[14]

Our relationship to food has become abstract—we increasingly live at a distant remove from the sources of sustenance, and hence in ignorance of the limits and demands of those sources, as well as the costs of our ignorance. "Most people now are living on the far side of a broken connection, and this is potentially catastrophic. Most people are now fed, clothed, and sheltered from sources, in nature and in the work of other

Charles Fish, *In Good Hands: the Keeping of a Family Farm* (New York: Farrar, Straus and Giroux, 1995), 102–03.

14 Berry, "Conservation is Good Work," in *Sex, Economy, Freedom and Community* (New York: Pantheon Books, 1993), 37.

}111{

people, toward which they feel no gratitude and exercise no responsibility."[15]

Our "fast food nation"—as has been remarkably documented in a book of that title by Eric Schlosser—has systematically sought to eliminate small family farming and non-standardized production in favor of factory farming fueled by poor and uneducated immigrant labor.[16] Humans lose all sense of the natural cycle of life and death; animals are treated with cruelty and enormous suffering. Meanwhile, the structure of our landscape has been altered to make the procurement of convenient food all the more convenient—endless highways and parking lots at the expense of the sidewalks and storefronts of downtowns. We treat animals and all of nature like a vast "filling station," and eat accordingly. While, in my view, meat-eating in a cultured and civilized fashion reflects and attests to human ascent, in its current social setting, meat-eating increasingly represents a return to barbarity.[17] Forgotten has been the Biblical call for stewardship, in which animals and nature are not treated as mere instruments of human convenience, but with respect and dignity in recognition of the way in which we, too, are creatures of infirmity and need.[18]

If democracy's rise accompanied the universal use of the fork, it may very well be that the increasing disuse of the fork corresponds to democracy's decline and fall. While one of democracy's prevailing tendencies is to dismiss *forms*—to embrace informality in all instances—democracy, in fact, is in need precisely of forms to prevent its self-destruction.

15 Berry, "In Distrust of Movements," in *Citizenship Papers* (Washington, DC: Shoemaker & Hoard, 1993), 48.

16 Eric Schlosser, *Fast Food Nation: The Dark Side of the All-American Meal* (New York: Harper Perennial, 2002).

17 See Roger Scruton's eloquent defense of meat-eating in his essay "Eating Our Friends," in *A Political Philosophy: Arguments for Conservatism* (New York: Continuum US, 2006), 47–63. On this general topic see also his essay "A Righter Shade of Green," in *The American Conservative* (July 16, 2007).

18 A particularly eloquent call to stewardship deriving from the Biblical and Christian tradition has been articulated by former G. W. Bush speechwriter Matthew Scully in his book *Dominion: The Power of Man, the Suffering of Animals, and the Call to Mercy* (New York: St. Martin's, 2003).

Informality represents our impatience with law; convenience reflects our acquiescence to desire and appetite. Our harsh and hateful political culture reflects the decline of civility—of forms. Democracy, properly understood, is a really an elaborate form of table manners in which disparate and *hungry* people sit down together and "agree" to control their appetites. Based upon conversation—upon speech—democracy requires us to take sufficient time to speak, and more importantly, to *listen*. The fork and knife do not "help" us to eat so much as hinder us from eating too quickly; likewise, democracy rightly conceived forces us to slow down. Democracy is not about *efficiency*, but rather, about fostering productive inefficiency. If the fork is the greatest technology in the realm of food, certainly the most dazzling technological advances in the domain of politics is *Robert's Rules of Order*. That stunning apparatus slows debate, gums up the works, and most importantly, forces debate; yet, it also gives us a way to end debate and to make a decision. Politics—and democracy especially—like eating with manners, is not about convenience and efficiency, but rather about learning self-restraint and self-governance. Responding to calls for more "efficiency" and "expertise" in government, the great intellectual historian Christopher Lasch has objected that instead we should "defend democracy not as the most efficient but as the most *educational* form of government, one that extends the circle of debate as widely as possible and thus forces all citizens to articulate their views, to put their views at risk, and to cultivate the virtues of eloquence, clarity of thought and expression, and sound judgment."[19] Politics permits the gathering of humans not in order to commit violence upon each other, but to foster a common life starting in civility but culminating with friendship and love. When people complain that this or that decision is "just politics," I respond, and thank goodness too—for, it is politics that makes us most human. He who is without a city is either a beast or a god.

Beasts and gods—humans are neither. And yet, nor can we reject the part of us that partakes of both. To deny our nature as animals would

---

19 Christopher Lasch, "The Lost Art of Argument," in *The Revolt of the Elites and the Betrayal of Democracy* (New York: W.W. Norton & Company, 1995), 171.

mean to starve. Yet, we starve too if we deny humanity's participation in divinity. Inherent in those very practices that we develop in order to ascend from violence and bestiality, those customs that make us most human, is a sign of our hunger for more. In lifting our heads above the horizon, in rising above mere appetite, we experience wonder, awe, and curiosity about creation in all its manifold forms. The first sin of humanity—in which the serpent tempted Eve to eat of the apple so that "ye shall be as gods . . ."—is both a lamentable sign of humankind's inclination to crave to be more than we should rightly wish, but too it hints at humanity's praiseworthy longing for communion with the divine. We were forced from Eden and became meat-eaters. We were cursed to "eat the bread from the sweat of our own brow": to know what it is to provide for ourselves and to learn the arts of food preparation and proper eating. We formed cities and civilizations, and developed customs specific to each city and each religion. We became human, and in becoming human, strove to know God.

Yet, in our specificity and difference, our particularity and parochialism enacts into the fabric of daily life a reminder of our non-parochial and universal beginning. As Leon Kass has written, through our rituals surrounding food and its preparation and consumption, we sanctify eating as a memorial to human creation. We seek to feed our souls as much as our bodies. And this particular hunger we enact every time we participate in the Lord's supper. One of the central mysteries of my—for many, our—faith is the transubstantiation of bread and wine into the body and blood of Christ Jesus. Flannery O'Connor said, "if it's just a symbol, then to hell with it." She was responding to one defense against the charge that Christian mass was a barbarism in which people enacted cannibalism. And, in a way, that's what it is: we do eat the body and drink the blood of Christ. But, by doing so, I eat in a form wholly contrary to the motivations behind cannibalism: I do not submit to mere appetite; by eating, I celebrate their defeat. I do not eat from a hunger that drives me to eat; I eat so that I may hunger. If humanity's first sin is to eat so that we may become gods, in the Lord's supper one eats to become fully human. And centrally part of becoming human is to take within me the divine who was himself completely human.

Thus we see the sense of W. H. Auden's full refrain about the relationship of food and the divine: "The slogan of Hell: Eat or be eaten. The slogan of Heaven: Eat *and* be eaten."[20]

This chapter began as a lecture to a group of students in Oxford during a summer Honors Program sponsored by the Intercollegiate Studies Institute. The theme of the summer program was "Manners and Morals," and the topic of the lecture was inspired by some banter with my oldest son, who was a young boy at the time. I delivered the lecture at Oriel College in the summer of 2004. I count it as among my favorite, and best-received lectures, and I still regularly draw from it in various classroom lectures.

The lecture was subsequently posted on the I.S.I. website, where it was read by, among others, the legendary Fr. James V. Schall of Georgetown University. I later became Fr. Schall's colleague at Georgetown University, and he would regularly praise this talk when I would pass him in the halls of the department. Years later I was invited to contribute to a Festschrift for Schall, and decided that this essay would be an appropriate way to honor him. It appeared in Jerusalem, Athens, and Rome: Essays in Honor of James V. Schall, S.J., *edited by Marc Guerra, and published in 2013 by Augustine Press.*

---

20   Auden, *A Certain World,* 134.

Chapter 6
Progress and Memory:
Making Whole Our Historical Sense

I. Introduction: Temporal Unity and Disunity:
The Problem of Modernity

Time present and time past
Are both perhaps present in time future,
And time future contained in time past . . .

—T. S. Eliot, *The Four Quartets*

I want to address the human experience of time, and in particular
what I will refer to as the full horizon of temporality. This phenomenon—time experienced simultaneously and continuously in its full dimension—is perhaps the decisively unique feature about human beings,
the thing that makes us a distinctive creature among the creatures. More
than our opposable thumb, our corresponding ability to use tools, or our
capacity for language, our upright posture or our intellectual formida-
bleness, it is our distinct capacity to *experience and act consciously
within* the whole of the temporal spectrum—past, present, and future—
that makes us a distinct creature among creatures. It is our capacity consciously and freely to carry with us the past and to anticipate and even
to an extent shape different possible futures that in some sense "acti-
vates" all of our other capacities—speech, tool-making, and so on.

While I do not know what goes on in the consciousness of other
creatures, based upon their external behavior it seems evident that most
creatures function primarily in the present tense. Yes, it's true that creatures seem to remember certain things—my dog knows by smell when

we're close to the house of a Dalmatian he finds particularly loathsome—and that they anticipate, as seems to be the case each Spring when birds work assiduously to build their nests. Yet, these behaviors would seem to be functions of instinct rather than reflection—automatic responses that are not the function of reflection about a knowledge of the past and reasonably formed expectations about the future that allow certain plans and anticipations that are likely to result in certain future arrangements, or many possible futures depending upon our free choices in the present. Even as my dog "remembers" the scent of the Dalmatian's yard or the bird "anticipates" the future by building a nest, what's noteworthy about these seeming expressions of memory and anticipation is that the actions taken by these creatures could not be different. They act automatically, without reflection or choice—they are most fundamentally creatures of the present moment.

What is singularly unique about human beings is our capacity for free choice *informed* by our knowledge of the past and in anticipation of the likely impact of our choices upon the future. If other creatures live predominantly in the *present*, humans are unique in their capacity to bring both the past and the future *into the present*. Humans live in the present—as creatures we live always in a fleeting moment of time between past and future—but through faculties of memory and the ability to plan for the future, we accumulate the past within the present and draw the future into our own moment, stepping purposefully and consciously into future time with a large inheritance from the past.

Our experience of the *presence* of the past and the future is expressed and felt most fully in our knowledge of continuity of *generations*—the memory of those who have preceded us, and our anticipation of those who will follow us. Recalling those who have preceded and awaiting those who will follow, we forge civilization itself, the accumulation of memory and the intention of continuity into the future. Unique human capacities orient us to the past and future within our present, including especially gratitude to what we have inherited and a corresponding sense of obligation for the safe passage of our inheritance into the future. Unlike the beasts, as civilized creatures we bring the past and the future into our present when we memorialize and call to mind those who are no longer with us—especially in song, story and prayer—and when we preserve a good dwelling place for those who follow, from the painting of the nursery walls to the conveyance of stories, song and prayer to our children and to theirs. If conservatism is anything, it is the effort to maintain the close linking and continuity of time, of the past and the future always embedded in the present.

If humanity is most fully human when fully experiencing all three temporal dimensions, then I would like to suggest that the distinctive feature of *modernity* has been *the fracturing of the temporal horizon*. While modernity can be defined and understood in many ways—as a scientific revolution, a theological transformation, an economic watershed, an epistemological sea-change—I'd like to argue that what underlies many of these various features of modernity (in its various iterations) is a *fracturing* and segregation of the human experience of time. In particular, I would like to argue that modernity is tripartite—a contestation of three worldviews—each of which stakes its claim to human allegiance based upon an emphasis on *one* temporal dimension, whether the present, the future, or the past. Three competing worldviews have coalesced around one of these temporal moments: *liberalism* tends toward experiencing life and the world in the *present*; *progressivism* (of various sorts, including Communism) sees the culmination of humanity's and the world's possibilities in the *future*; and *nostalgism* dons rose-tinted glasses in its high regard for a perfected *past*. These three iterations of modernity—tending toward one temporal dimension—are, admittedly, ideal types, but reveal not only the defining aspect of the several faces of modernity, but the deepest *pathology* of modernity in its radical obscuring of the fullness of time—and may help us see not only what conservatism is NOT, but what it IS.

II. Liberalism: Living in the Present

Modernity is inaugurated by the recommendation that we shatter the human possibility of living within the full spectrum of time. It begins with a radical rejection of the past as a source of wisdom and counsel, of caution and limits, and also a corresponding neglect of the future as a time unknowable if little can be carried from the past. It is inaugurated by the commendation to live in the *present tense*, with particular force by the philosophers Thomas Hobbes and John Locke, in the philosophy we know to be called *liberalism*.

Liberalism begins with a radical critique of the ancestral. The philosophy of Hobbes and Locke—along with other modernist philosophers such as Descartes and Kant—begins by indicting the legitimacy of the *inherited*, which is to say, the unchosen. That which is bequeathed us from the past is understood to be a form of generational oppression, arbitrary rule of those who happened to be born before we were. Liberalism inaugurates a project in legitimacy that can only be conferred upon a human institution when that institution has been *chosen*. It rejects the ruling claims of tradition as arbitrary impositions, instead holding that every generation should in some sense understand itself to create the world anew through its own choices—indeed, displacing the ancestral for the governance of the current and up-to-date. It was the French political theorist Bertrand de Jouvenel who, assessing the basic psychology of liberal philosophy, argued that liberal theory derived from "childless men who must have forgotten their childhood."

The anthropology of early liberal theory conceives of the human creature as a creature of appetite and fear, of will and cowardice, of desire and avoidance. The human creature is above all driven by *pleasure* and *pain*, seeking out opportunities for corporeal enjoyment and avoiding confrontations that may result in bodily suffering. We are creatures whose existence is largely defined in material terms, whose aim of life is the achievement of bodily comfort and the minimization of corporeal unpleasantness. Thus, Hobbes would argue that the aim of human society—once it comes into existence—is the achievement of *"commodious living,"* while Locke argued that a main aim of human life is "indolency of the body." The main wellspring of human activity is self-interest, and self-interest above all is connected to accumulating pleasures and avoiding pains of the body.

Of course, liberalism would not be as powerfully influential a philosophy if it were not at least half-true, and the truth of liberalism's half-truth that most fundamentally persuades is the fact that we are indeed bodies—separate and isolated from one another, feeling only our own pains and pleasures, ultimately entering and leaving the world alone and experiencing the world solely through our own consciousness.

Liberalism reduces the human experience to the experience of bodies—our own bodies—and thus disconnects us not only psychically from other bodies in motion, but from a lineage of other creatures that preceded and follow us. The scientific theory in the backdrop is Galilean and eventually Newtonian physics, the interpretation of the universe as one of many bodies in motion, moved by utterly predictable and irresistible forces—gravity for planets, self-interest for humans. Human society is to be shaped and formed in the wake of an understanding of our own individuated experience as desiring and fearful bodies. We are reduced increasingly to a single point—not only corporeal dots on a map, but *temporally* as monadic moments of the present, sensitive to pleasure and pain, attracted to comfort in the now-time.

The anthropology of liberalism divorces us from time past and time future. Humans are de-cultured and a-historical creatures: in the State of Nature there is only Now-time, absent culture or memory, history or planning. We are by nature non-cultural creatures. Even as we enter society—giving some thought to the future by means of a social contract—we maintain the kernel of our individual and separate corporeality. If we owe obligations to our fellow man (and, truth be told, we're so prone to break the contract given our preferences for the pleasures of NOW, we agree to set up a powerful overseer who will assure swift punishment to those who transgress the terms of the contract), it is by dint of the contract we explicitly or implicitly signed in the interests of increasing our pleasure and decreasing our pain. Our lives are complicated by interactions with other humans, but all relations and institutions are subject to the logic of voluntarism—the free choice of individuals. We can make and re-make society and all human relations on the basis of human choice. The claims of the ancestral—of the past—are to exert no preferential claim upon us. John Locke even tells us that the logic of choice must inform the relations of families: children reaching the age of maturity owe no particular obligation or gratitude to their parents, and husband and wife who have raised their children are free to dissolve their marital contract and move on. We are to live in the now-time, unburdened by the weight of generations past and future, free to be you and me, a choice-machine whose primary objective is maximization of pleasure and elimination of pain.

The economics of liberalism is market capitalism, an economic system designed to undergird our pursuit of corporeal pleasure and reduction bodily pain. It is an economics populated by human choosers —utility maximizers—who exist in a world governed by the Present Tense. Having no past and knowing that in the long run we are all dead, it is an economics that regards the world as available for current use— and, indeed, understands that anything unused and unenjoyed today will be used for the personal enjoyment of someone else tomorrow. Better to use it today for the pleasure of my own body than to leave it to the pleasure of some body that is not mine. Because past and future do not exist, forms of gratitude and obligation are irrelevant to my calculation. The older obligation of stewardship—which is to say, thoughtfulness about the impact of my actions upon the future based upon my knowledge of the past—is replaced by the faith in the Market, and in particular, faith in the inventive ability of the future to deal with the costs and consequences of my self-interest today. A mechanism justifying thoughtless consumption replaces the obligation and duty of thoughtfulness.

Its politics is liberal democracy—a politics designed to promote maximum individual freedom, protection of rights, minimal public or private obligation, ever-increasing mobility and opportunity. Among its great innovations is the invention of modern representation, a vehicle that relieves citizens of the obligation of having to think about much beyond themselves and their interests. The intention of the designers of liberal democracy was that representatives—reflecting an older ethic of obligation to past and future – would be safeguards and stewards of the common good. However, absent the fostering of any such attention among those who would be *electing* those representatives, the unsurprising reality has been that the overwhelming demand for satiation of pleasures and avoidance of pain *in the present tense* advantage representatives who promise to act on behalf of satiation *NOW*. The language of sacrifice in the name of gratitude to the past or obligation to the future disappears from our public vocabulary, and the language of the *present* comes to dominate—particularly the invocation of Rights and Entitlements, invoked by electorates who threaten punishment to those who would deny our enjoyment of the Now.

Liberalism is evidently humane because it provides exceedingly well to people who are now alive. But it caused a violent reaction by those who think it too ignoble, too materialistic, too self-interested and too exploitative. The triumph of Liberalism—and its impetus to live in the Present Tense—gave rise to Progressivism, and its aspiration for a better future.

III. Progressivism: Living in the Future

Progressivism regarded in dim light the achievements of liberalism. Discontent with its emphasis on animal satisfaction, it sought to place the human condition on a higher plane—in contrast to that of self-interest, instead one of *disinterest* or even *universal love*; instead of material satiation, the transcendence of the merely corporeal; instead of the stress upon individual rights, the achievement of universal Right. Yet, progressivism acknowledged that it sought a condition yet-unseen in the history and existence of humankind. It sought, then, a realization and culmination of some future condition, a fundamental change and transformation of the human creature, at least in part accurately understood by liberalism, into something wholly new and yet unknown.

Progressivism's anthropology is premised upon *change*. If liberalism regards human nature as unchanging—always and everywhere predictably motivated by self-interest, as much a feature of the natural law of humans as the natural laws of gravity move the heavenly spheres—then progressivism by contrast regards the only permanent feature of the human creature to be change, and that the direction of change is necessarily toward improvement and progress. If liberalism is informed by the science of Newtonian physics, then progressivism takes its cue from the science of Darwinian biology.

According to progressivism, the human creature is constantly evolving, transforming, progressing, coming ever closer to perfection. The path of humanity is that of an upward trajectory, ever-better, ever-improved. Progressivism arose as a response to a discontent with liberalism and its unchanging view of human nature. Thinkers like Condorcet and Comte, and later John Stuart Mill, Karl Marx, and in America John Dewey argued that humanity was demonstrably better now than in the past, and based upon a trajectory that could be projected forward indefinitely, would be better still in the future, and perhaps—not unrealistically—potentially perfect at a point in a foreseeable future time.

Progressivism thus not only—like Liberalism—discounted the past, it also discounted the Present. Progressivism understood that the present was always in the process of becoming the Past, and thus, inherently inferior to the future. It lived philosophically, politically and economically in a future time, although even in its present it projected what that future would look like and sought—even in the present—to accelerate the process of progressive improvement. Progressivism's self-awareness of the future as a better time justified its manipulation of the Present in order to accelerate the arrival of the Future. Whether the call for revolution by the proletariat by Marx, the justification of imperialism of backward races or rule by intellectual elites by Mill, or Dewey's argument that nature should be subject to human interrogation and torture in an effort to "extract" its secrets for human employment and use, Progressivism was more Machiavellian than Machiavelli, arguing that any means justified a discernibly perfected end.

If human self-interest was an obstacle to the apotheosis of a better future, then self-interest must be overcome. For Marx, self-interest was the obstacle to the attainment of our truer perception of our "species-being," as for Mill and Dewey the assumptions of self-interest that underpinned liberal democracy were an obstacle to the culmination of a "religion of humanity." If liberalism put all human institutions on the footing of choice—even the family—Progressivism regarded all such institutions as fundamentally illegitimate, partial expressions of our true social and even "cosmic" consciousness. Thus Progressivism set in its sights all partial and intermediary institutions, whether marriage, family, church, fraternal association, neighborhood, partial political units such as the States, even and ultimately the Nation itself. In the end all such partial allegiances were to be dissolved in favor of the universal embrace of humanity itself, and thus—in the name of the Future—efforts to accelerate the dissolution of those partial associations were justified in the Present. The Present was to make itself obsolete in the name of bringing about more quickly the Kingdom of Heaven on Earth.

Progressivism almost universally holds a set of economic commitments that reflect confidence in a future condition in which human self-interest has been overcome, and thereby justifies elimination of any remnants of such economic self-interest in the Present. Private property is the most visible and evident sign of partiality and self-interest, and ultimately must be eliminated in the name of common ownership and the overcoming of the self and its partial commitments. However, because of strong residual expressions of antiquarian self-interest, there is the acknowledgment among Progressives that an intermediary period of severe and even despotic government is needed that will precede a future apotheosis when all government will cease to exist. Because human self-interest itself will be eliminated, there will be no more need for government because politics itself will cease to exist. Evidence for that future condition of self-overcoming exists sufficiently among the more Progressed classes to justify rule by the Vanguard of the society. Thus, a thinker like John Stuart Mill wrote, "that whenever it ceases to be true that mankind, as a rule, prefer themselves to others, and those nearest to them to those more remote, from that moment Communism is not only practicable, but the only defensible form of society; and will, when that time arrives, be assuredly carried into effect. For my own part, not believing in universal selfishness, I have no difficulty in admitting that Communism would even now be practicable among the elite of mankind, and may become so among the rest."

Progressives know enough of the trajectory of history—are already at least theoretically or prospectively already living in the future—that they can differentiate between the more and the less progressed. Progressivism—while officially committed to a thoroughly egalitarian future—justifies illiberal and inegalitarian political arrangements in the *present* in the name of a better future. Egalitarianism is posited as a desirable future condition, an aspiration that justifies the beneficent and paternalistic rule of sufficiently progressed elites in the Present. Thus, in a somewhat progressed and civilized nation like England, J. S. Mill argues that the educated elite should receive more votes than the unwashed masses, and especially that the mark of sufficient progress will be those persons who bear advanced degrees and signs of higher education. However, for those more backward nations that still exist in a state of "barbarism," more severe forms of elite rule are justified. As Mill wrote in his work *Representative Government*,

> a people in a state of savage independence . . . is practically incapable of making any progress in civilisation until it has learnt to obey. The indispensable virtue, therefore, in a government which establishes itself over a people of this sort is, that it make itself obeyed. To enable it to do this, the constitution of the government must be nearly, or quite, despotic. A constitution in any degree popular, dependent on the voluntary surrender by the different members of the community of their individual freedom of action, would fail to enforce the first lesson which the pupils, in this stage of their progress, require. Accordingly, the civilisation of such tribes, when not the result of juxtaposition with others already civilised, is almost always the work of an absolute ruler, deriving his power either from religion or military prowess; very often from foreign arms.
>
> Such uncivilised races, and the bravest and most energetic still more than the rest, are averse to continuous labour of an unexciting kind. Yet all real civilisation is at this price; without such labour, neither can the mind be disciplined into the habits required by civilised society, nor the material world prepared to receive it. There needs a rare concurrence of circumstances, and for that reason often a vast length of time, to reconcile such a people to industry, unless they are for a while compelled to it. Hence even *personal slavery*, by giving a commencement to industrial life, and enforcing it as the exclusive occupation of the most numerous portion of the community, may accelerate the transition to a better freedom than that of fighting and rapine.[1]

---

1   John Stuart Mill, "On Representative Government," in *On Liberty, Utilitarianism and Other Essays*, ed. Mark Philp and Frederick Rosen (New York: Oxford University Press, 2015), 232.

Of course, Progressives encounter claims among those who must be forced to be progressed that they are relatively content in their way of life—for example, enjoy the condition in which marriage, family, church and community are centers of human existence—but such content-ment—to those who have knowledge of the future condition of mankind—is known to the Progressive to be a form of false conscious-ness, a form of self-deception that is the result of insufficient knowledge of the future. The claim that there are those who know better than some what is good for them is the result of the knowledge of an anticipated life in the Future and efforts on the part of those in the Present for its acceleration. Among the solutions offered out of paternalistic care by Progressives during the heyday of Progressivism were eugenic policies that sought to improve and accelerate the process of species advance-ment, including forced sterilization of the mentally feeble and inferior and barbaric races, as well as manipulation of reproduction to produce ever more perfected children.

This certainty about the contours of the future, and the accompanying certainty that its culmination will necessarily result from and justify cer-tain drastic efforts in the present, is best characterized as the disposition of *optimism*. Optimism in this more modern sense is a disposition not only of certainty about the shape of the future, but bold confidence that one's actions in the Present will bring about the culmination of history's trajectory. It is a confident and assertive view toward the future that tends to dismiss the reality of "unintended consequences" as irrelevant or fun-damentally unreal. It overlooks present suffering in the name of future, and is supremely self-assured that a stance of superior progressivity jus-tifies the rule and even despotism by elites in achieving the universal con-dition of a perfected Future. Optimism is a near-impervious disposition that dismisses not only the reality of contingency and uncertainty, but most fundamentally the imperfection and imperfectability of humankind. Thus, all apparent setbacks are actually advances and evidence to the con-trary justify redoubling efforts by the more Progressed classes to seek ad-vancement. Thus, a philosophy that is severely critical of the past age of religious faith is subject to a faith in the future so unshakeable that it de-nies the relevance of any evidence that would contradict that faith, much less recommend circumspection, caution, and even humility.

IV. Nostalgism: Living in the Past

There is a third form of temporal fragmentation that constitutes one of the features of the landscape of modernity, and is not only a reaction *against* Progressivism, but is in nearly all respects the flip-side or the photo-negative of Progressivism. Often confused as conservatism, it is in fact something quite distinct—a radicalization of the conservative impulse, one that evinces not the modest and cautious disposition of conservatism, but the radicalism of the reverse revolutionist. It is a belief that the human creature ought to live in the past tense, and is best captured by the label "*nostalgism.*" Nostalgia is a word of relatively recent coinage, dating back to the nineteenth century and combining two Greek words, "*nostos,*" which means "homecoming," and *algos*, which means roughly "a longing for that which is absent." These words are ancient, but nostalgia itself is a modern phenomenon, a response to the modern shattering of our full temporal horizon.

Progressivism holds that humankind is an ever-improving creature and optimistically posits that the future is the temporal dimension in which the fullness and excellence of human life will be achieved. By contrast, nostalgism holds that humankind is in a continual process of *decline* and *regress*, that various corruptions have caused a falling away from a previously better condition, and that the fullness and excellence of human life existed at some definite point in the *Past*. Nostalgists are prone to the opposite disposition of the optimism of Progressives, namely *pessimism*, the view that things are getting worse and it's unlikely that the downward spiral of *disimprovement* or decline can be reversed (at best it might be slowed). However, positing the existence of a time when the human creature lived in near-perfect happiness and contentment—like that future time that is imagined by Progressives—Nostalgists at their most radical assume a hostile and even revolutionary stance toward the Present and the Future in which extreme actions are justified in getting us *back*. And, that point in the past—the very mirror image of that point in the future for the Progressive—is a moment of lost perfection, of complete un-alienation and pre-political (as opposed to post-political) equality and liberty.

Like Progressives, Nostalgists despise the imperfection of the Present and posit instead a perfect moment in another time—this time, the

Past, not the Future. However, Progressives have the advantage of imagining a perfect future that cannot be disproven in advance, while Nostalgists seek to draw from a past that is in many respects known to us,
and thus subject to disillusion. Nostalgism thus is as much a condition
in which we seek to forget or obscure, ignore or minimize whatever parts
of the past may contradict an idealized version of it. The Nostalgist is,
curiously, as likely to be as hostile to the lessons of history as the Progressive, given that history is at least always as much the recollection of
human failure and misery and tragedy as it is of human happiness and
satisfaction. Nostalgism involves a kind of willful forgetting, as Progressivism involves a kind of willful imagining.

The first great Nostalgist was Jean-Jacques Rousseau, especially
Rousseau of the First and Second Discourses. In the First Discourse
Rousseau developed his critique of Progressivism, in which he resisted
the spirit of the age by answering in the negative the following question
in an essay contest: "Has the restoration of the sciences and arts tended
to purify morals?" Rousseau argued that nearly every "advance" of the
Age of Enlightenment in the sciences and the arts had led to a decline
of morals, and posited that this decline could be attributed not merely to
his contemporaries in the Enlightenment movement, but dates as far back
as rise of the arts, sciences, philosophy and other achievements of the
Athenians. Unfashionably, Rousseau defended the superiority of the
Spartans, those people who were otherwise uninfected by the corruption
of hyper-self-reflection, the preciousness of the arts, the purported superiority of the educated elite, the condescension of the proto-Progres-
sive mindset. Exhibiting the more solid virtues of commonweal and
military solidarity, the Spartans were largely undifferentiated, identifying
exclusively with the clan and city, and denying any reality to human individuality or uniqueness. Rousseau—as is wont with Nostalgists—in
the *Second Discourse* revised his estimate of when the ideal moment of
human existence had occurred in the past, placing it in a literally pre-
historical time when humans were really no different than animals (thus,
living entirely in the PRESENT, a condition that had occurred in the
PAST), before civilization, society, culture, even language and differentiation of selfhood. Being unbothered by the ravages of self-conscious-
ness, anxiety, envy, and fear of death, it was a time in which humans

were satisfied with mere instinct fulfillment and thus content and in a sense happy. While Rousseau denied that there was any going back to this original condition of basic satisfaction, his life-long project was the effort to "re-create" basic features of this condition, to bring us back (now by means of elaborate design, whether politically through the Social Contract or individually through an education like that of Emile) to a condition of contentment through the overcoming of human alienation and the attendant miseries of civilization.

If the scientific theory undergirding Liberalism was Newtonian physics, and that underpinning Progressivism is Darwinism, then the scientific theory that underpins Nostalgism is that theory developed by Lord Kelvin, namely the Entropic inevitability of the universe's dissipation that is destined according to the Second Law of Thermodynamics. Every seeming advance of progress, by this understanding, is in fact a kind of "regress," or an acceleration of dissipation, decay and corruption. A thinker such as Henry Adams—whose late writings were almost exclusively devoted to applying the insight of Kelvin's Second Law to history—saw in the "progress" of America following the Civil War—and the attendant embrace of Darwinism in celebration of humankind's inevitable march of progress—as signs of decline and reason for pessimism about the future. Turning first to a better past represented by better ancestors, and then turning to the medieval cathedrals of France and the worship of Mary as the last best moment of wholeness and genuine human feeling, he idealized the Past over Present and Future, turning his back on each as irredeemably degraded.

Like Rousseau and Adams, Martin Heidegger also exhibited the Nostalgist impulse in his late writings devoted to the critique of technology as a curse that undermined true human experience of the world, and in other writing that saw the poetic peasant life of Southern Germany as the authentic alternative to modern alienation. "The threat to man does not come in the first instance from the potentially lethal machines and apparatus of technology," Heidegger wrote in his famous essay "The Question of Technology." Rather, "the actual threat has already threatened man in his essence, . . . [threatening him] with the possibility that it could be denied to him to enter into a more original revealing and hence to experience the call of a more primal truth" (309). Technology is not most fundamentally to be judged based upon its constructive or destructive potential to cause harm to the Present or to the Future, but in obscuring from us an *original* "revealing" and "more primal truth" that existed in the PAST.

The Nostalgist's ideal past moment tends to recede ever further into the past, ultimately (like Rousseau) finding a resting place in a pre-history that precedes the emergence of human consciousness. Politically, Nostalgism is pre-political and economically it tends to be pre-economic, or at least portrays a past before the conventions of money and superfluous professions. It is seen at times today in the anti-human stance of radicals in the Environmental movement, those who would wish away the existence of humanity (reflected in the popularity of books like Alan Weisman's *The World Without Us,* whose cover portrays buildings with corresponding "reflections" of plants), and shows like National Geographic's *When Humans Disappear*. One sees it in the Prius car commercial in which the car—built out of sticks, twine and grass—is shown in time-acceleration to decompose and leave no mark upon the pristine ground on which it was constructed. Politically and economically, today a certain kind of Nostalgism is seen in a powerful combination of anti-humanism and environmentalism that accepts fully the modern and liberal notion that human society is antithetical to—opposite of—nature, but instead of siding with the human undertaking to conquer nature, envisions the elimination of humankind in favor of a humanless nature.

V. Restoring Temporal Continuity

What is needed in our time, of course, is a restoration of the lived human reality of temporal fullness—the felt-presence of past and future in the present. As T. S. Eliot wrote in *The Four Quartets,*

Here between the hither and farther shore
While time is withdrawn, consider the future
And the past with an equal mind.

The conditions of modernity have made our relationship with the past and future deeply troubled, made us apt to live either principally in the present, or to view the future with optimism or the past with nostalgia.

These temporal dispositions—optimism and nostalgia—are features of a modern inheritance that feed off each other while obscuring a better relationship of the full temporal horizon.

There are, however, more *conservative* dispositions toward the past and the future that, rather than seeking to effect a temporal disruption—by privileging either the past or the future, or insisting upon the fierce urgency of NOW—rather draw closely together the past, present and future in a concurrent continuum. Those dispositions—in contrast to nostalgia and optimism—are instead *MEMORY* and *HOPE*.

It was the intellectual historian Christopher Lasch who clarified better than anyone these respective dispositions toward the past and future, memory and hope. In his magisterial book entitled *The True and Only Heaven: Progress and its Critics*, which is a study of the anti-progressive tradition in American political thought (and includes a more admiring chapter on Reinhold Niebuhr, among many others)—Lasch began by showing that optimism and nostalgia were flip-sides of the same coin—"Just as the idea of progress has the curious effect of weakening the inclination to make intelligent provision for the future, nostalgia—its ideological twin—undermines the ability to make intelligent use of the past." More importantly still, Lasch showed how their better alternatives—memory and hope—forged a continuity between past, present and future, rather than their rupture.

In contrast to nostalgia—which involves a willful form of forgetting—*memory* is an honest recollection of the past, a full reckoning of that great resource of accumulated time that constitutes the great storehouse of human history. Yet, unlike so much of contemporary history-study—which consists in a debunking—memory recalls good and bad alike, recognizing that the one cannot be dissociated from the other and therefore always recalling to mind that the human condition in this saeculum is always imperfectible. Here is Lasch:

> Nostalgic representations of the past evoke a time irretrievably lost and for that reason timeless and unchanging. Strictly speaking, nostalgia does not entail the exercise of memory at all, since the past it idealizes stands outside of time, frozen in unchanging perfection. Memory too may idealize the past,

but not in order to condemn the present. It draws hope and comfort from the past in order to enrich the present and to face what comes with good cheer. It sees past, present and future as continuous. It is less concerned with loss than with our continuing indebtedness to a past the formative influence of which lives on in our patterns of speech, our gestures, our standards of honor, our expectations, our basic disposition toward the world around us.[2]

Noteworthy in this passage about *memory* is the invocation of *hope*: that a properly oriented memory supplies us, in addition to a proper attitude of indebtedness and gratitude, the resources to appropriately face the future. And, that appropriate disposition to the future—hope, in contrast to optimism—in turn supplies us with a confidence that the past can serve as a proper and meet guide. Again, Lasch:

> Hope does not demand a belief in progress. It demands a belief in justice: a conviction that the wicked will suffer, that wrongs will be made right, that the underlying order of things is not flouted with impunity. Hope implies a deep-seated trust in life that appears absurd to those who lack it. It rests on confidence not so much in the future as in the past. It derives from the earliest memories . . . in which the experience of order and contentment was so intense that subsequent disillusionments cannot dislodge it. Such experience leaves as its residue the unshakeable conviction, not that the past was better than the present, but that trust is never completely misplaced, even though it is never completely justified either and therefore destined inevitably to disappointments.[3] (80–81)

Such continuity of past, present and future is not the result of individual concentration or sheer will-power, but the lived reality of a

2   Christopher Lasch, *The True and Only Heaven: Progress and Its Critics* (New York: W. W. Norton & Company, 1991), 82–83.
3   Lasch, *The True and Only Heaven,* 80–81.

properly constituted *culture*. Indeed, it could legitimately be argued that this is the paramount task of culture and reason for its existence—to draw close together the disparate temporal dimensions that may otherwise be prone to become separated, unrelated, and strangers to one another. The inauguration of political modernity through liberalism begins with an assault on culture—an aggressive critique of the legitimacy of "the ancestral" and a conception of human beings not constituted in and through culture, but as creatures that are naturally understood to be a-cultural and for whom culture is always foremost a *choice* and as subject to abandonment as initiation. The subsequent "waves" of modernity's temporal disruption I've described here—Progressivism and Nostalgism—are as equally hostile toward culture, with Progressivism arrayed against the institutions of memory and tradition as obstacles of progress, and the most radical Nostalgism wedded to an idea of a pre-conscious (and hence pre-cultural) human creature, or at the very least committed to an illusory culture as imagined as the whole of the past that is a creation not of memory, but of misplaced reimaginings.

The conservative disposition *conserves* time in its full dimension—past, present, and future—and above all defends those forms of culture that provide safe transmission of the past through the present and into the indefinite future. Conservatism misunderstands itself when it considers itself as solely or exclusively about the past—though, of course, it gives a special pride of place, centrality and importance to inheritance, memory and tradition. It was none other than Burke who articulated the essential wholeness of time, positing—against the likes of Hobbes and Locke—that the social contract was not merely "a partnership between those who are living, but between those who are living, those who are dead, and those who are to be born."[4]

It is not only the knowledge of, and limits and caution suggested by the past that ought to exert powerful limits upon our inclination toward reckless innovation, but also our knowledge of and obligation toward the *future*. This point was made powerfully recently by the conservative philosopher Roger Scruton who made a case for why a deep concern for,

4   Edmund Burke, *Reflections on the Revolution in France*, ed. J.G.A. Pocock (Indianapolis, IN: Hackett Publishing Company, Inc., 1987), 85.

and protection of, the environment ought rightly to be the provenance of *conservatism*, not liberalism. Above all, he argued, contemporary economic arrangements informed deeply by liberalism (namely, market capitalism) is very good at providing prosperity for living beings—those people we regard as current signatories of the Social Contract—but is exceedingly poor at considering the claims and needs of the *unborn*. Contemporary economic arrangements provide a powerful incentive toward the "externalization of costs," the reduction of effort and attendant costs through such measures as massive consumption, planned obsolescence, mountains of waste and scandalous levels of indebtedness that will require future generations to pay down. Such externalization is less successful when pushed off on *living* humans (think Erin Brockovich), but a near-universal practice as a burden placed upon future generations. According to Scruton, it is conservatism's capacity to think not merely about the past, but to draw the future equally into the present, especially through a strong sense of the interconnection of gratitude and obligation among generations. Here is Scruton, from a lecture he delivered at Georgetown University in 2007 entitled "Conservatism as Conservation":

> So what is to stop us from externalizing our costs onto future generations? Within our own families, we recoil from doing such a thing. I don't want to dump the costs of my life on my son, even though I shall be dead when he feels them. Nor would I wish my grandchildren to pay the price of my selfishness . . . .
>
> Through the device of the trust, English and American law has been able to protect the interests of absent generations by compelling the current owners of property to set their own interests aside. The trustees of a bequest must respect the wishes of the testator and in so doing—by holding their own desires and present emergencies in abeyance— will serve the interests of future generations. This form of ownership, and the moral idea contained in it, ought to be regarded as defining the conservative approach. We don't solve environmental problems by abandoning our attachment to private property

or free enterprise, but we can make sure that these notions are shaped by the spirit of trusteeship.[5]

Along with the notion of trusteeship there is in addition the Christian ideal of "stewardship" that draws not only future generations into our temporal orbit, but all of God's creation. The repairing of the fullness of our temporal horizon introduces a beneficial form of care and responsibility into our interactions with the world and all of its creatures—including the millions yet unborn. It demands of us a high degree of *thoughtfulness* about what we are doing, a form of thoughtfulness that the modern disruption of temporal continuity has relieved us of, but which we can at this point in our history ill afford. As Pope Benedict XVI has recently argued, there is an intimate connection between how we treat the world and how we treat each other: "*The way humanity treats the environment influences the way it treats itself, and vice versa.*" A society that treats the natural world as a disposable resource for current pleasure is just as likely to treat its unborn children the same way. Conservatives who are justifiably dedicated to an ethic of life need to move away from a visceral hatred of "environmentalism" and understand the profound continuity of our treatment of nature and humanity and their relationship to our current forms of temporal disruption and discontinuity.

Ralph Waldo Emerson wrote in an essay entitled "The Conservative" that mankind is divided between two fundamental parties, those oriented toward the past and those toward the future—which he termed "the Party of Memory and the Party of Hope." Americans of various parties have for too long operated under a false notion that this statement was in some way true, and have falsely construed these two terms to mean more closely the parties of optimism and nostalgia. If conservatism is to have a future—in my view—it needs to be the Party of Memory *and* Hope, properly understood. By reconnecting past, present and future, we can begin to restore history to its proper place, between past and future in a present that experiences the whole of our temporal horizon in every

5   Roger Scruton, "A Righter Shade of Green," *American Conservative*: June 16, 2007.

moment—a present that is constantly turning the future into the past, and yet in which the past freely roams into our future. Time present and time past /Are both perhaps present in time future,/And time future contained in time past . . .

This chapter was originally a lecture that was delivered in July 2009 for an I.S.I. Summer Honors program. The program was devoted to "Meaning in History: Learning from the Past."

Chapter 7
What Is Conservatism?

Everyone has an opinion about conservatism today, not only its condition—which ranges between being "dead" according to Sam Tanenhaus to "resurgent" according to strident voices on talk radio—but of course, what conservatism IS. While the definition of conservatism is contested by onlookers as well as self-proclaimed conservatives themselves, after a relatively short period in the wilderness following the election of 2008, conservatism appears to have found its footing. Indeed, if there is one thing that the political Left and the political Right agree upon—and that's not very much—it's the basic definition of conservatism. Limited government. Low taxes. Free markets. Strong national defense. Judicial restraint. Individual liberty. Family Values. And so on.

Conservatism, in other words, is a political platform with about 12 main planks, a well-defined political program that can be implemented more or less through legislation and some key judicial appointments. It looks with fondness upon the defined list of legislative aims in the 1994 "Contract with America" and with even more fondness on the select aims and accomplishments of President Ronald Reagan. Conservatism is largely understood to be a political agenda that above all requires concentration on electoral victory and ascension to political power. Thus, while the previous thirty years have been understood to have been a period of prominence for conservatism in America—given the dominance by conservatives in national politics—since the congressional elections of 2006 and especially the presidential election of 2008, it has been understood as a time of conservative decline. Conservatism has thus been understood to be closely aligned with the fortunes of the Republican party.

I want to suggest today that this is a most *unconservative* view of conservatism, and particularly inasmuch as it does not conform to the deepest philosophic and intellectual sources of conservatism, and even contradicts conservatism's basic tenets. Indeed, to see "conservatism" mainly as an actionable political agenda is to contradict the very basis on which conservatism first arose as an articulated modern philosophy—mainly articulated by Edmund Burke—who opposed the notion that the solutions to social ills were mainly to be found in and through politics. This was the stance of the French revolutionaries whom Burke condemned for their efforts to achieve a kind of "mathematical" or ideological politics by means of which society could be transformed. Burke instead argued on behalf of conservatism as a *culture* and a way of life, not narrowly a political program. At the point in which even conservatives would view their prospects as bound up with their electoral fortunes, Burke would likely have concluded that conservatism had not only lost its way, but had ceased to understand itself.

To retrieve conservatism from its decidedly unconservative modern incarnation, it's necessary to undertake a characteristically conservative project—to examine the past, and especially the historical and philosophical underpinnings of conservative thought (and, for that matter, its liberal and revolutionary counterpart) in order to understand conservatism better and anew. While this would require a lengthy treatise to even adequately begin that project of reclamation, I am only able in this short space to offer a preliminary sketch outlining what such a recovery would look like—in particular what would be the main features of conservatism rightly understood, and some of the resources one would need to turn to. I especially want to point to how a fitting understanding of conservatism relates to law, if not always to the way in which law is studied and understood in contemporary times and especially in the law schools.

For the purposes of providing a set of defined guideposts, I will speak about four main thinkers and four main ideas from each that have contributed to the conservative tradition—and, additionally, I will offer four corresponding points of relevance to law. These are not meant to be exhaustive either of the broader and more expansive philosophies of these respective thinkers, nor of conservatism as a whole, but I think lay out some of the main features that would need to be considered in a true recovery of conservatism in our age. The four thinkers and concepts I will explore today are as follows:

1. First, Aristotle stressed that human society and politics must be based on a conception of the Good, which is itself ultimately discernible by reason in conformity with nature. Thus, Aristotle argued that the political order needed as fully as possible to be organized to assist its citizens to conform to that nature, and thus that law served in a primary role as a teacher to citizens.
2. Second, in response to the first great modern ideology—philosophical liberalism—the less well-known Italian thinker Giambattista Vico argued on behalf of the centrality and even *naturalness* of *culture* and its necessary role in making us human beings. He argued that law was derived from, and an affirmation of, human culture. Training in the law was through familiarity with the "sense of the community" (or, "the common law"), and thus relied upon education in prudence and in the liberal arts.
3. Third, in response to the second great modern ideology—progressivism, in the form of the French Revolution—Edmund Burke argued on behalf of the full spectrum of human temporality—past, present, and future—in properly evaluating and guiding human conduct. He insisted on the central place of generations in human self-understanding, and thus understood law to be a conduit of human wisdom from past to present to future.
4. Lastly, Alexis de Tocqueville, witnessing the maturation of the world's first liberal democracy, argued that it would above all need ways to retain what he called "forms," and what we might call "formalism." He warned against the tendency of equality to obliterate forms, and recommended the retention of various forms and formalities that could be reconciled, even if always in tension, with democracy. Among his practical recommendations, he saw the law as a main exemplar of forms for democratic citizens, and lawyers as the great defenders of forms and formality in modern democratic times, even as the one necessary remnant of an aristocratic culture that democratic equality sought to displace.

1. Virtue and the Good

First, and perhaps above all, conservatism involves a substantive commitment to a moral order that is discernible through human reason. That moral order—resting upon a conception of human nature that is, within some measure of individual flexibility and societal variety, nevertheless fixed and permanent—demands conformity by human beings in their formation and in their actions. This is to say, there is an objective condition of human good that is discernible through reflection, study and judgment, and human beings only flourish when they conform to that standard. For Aristotle, the attainment of human good was a condition of human flourishing, which he defined as "a being-at-work of the soul in accordance with virtue." This condition he called "happiness," by which he meant not the fleeting feeling of a good mood or the subjective condition of pleasure or joy, but an objective condition in which humans—to the extent possible to individuals within their contexts and their potentials—achieve the full flourishing of their humanness.

Virtue was mainly the result of a pre-rational form of "habituation" that took place primarily in the family, but which required the existence of a good, moral, and ongoing political order for both its existence and its capacity to habituate the young. Indeed, Aristotle went so far as to argue that without existing in the context of a good polity, the efforts of the family were apt to be unsuccessful (he went so far as to say family life without the benefits of a polity was like that of the society of the Cyclopes—who, recall, ate visitors raw for dinner). It is the first lawgiver, Aristotle argued, who taught humans to restrain their appetites—literally, he argued, showing us how to restrain ourselves in those most elemental and instinctive manifestations of human appetite, in those matters (he writes) relating to "eating and sex."

Virtue involves especially the practice of self-control, the capacity for self-government of appetite, whether individually or collectively. Virtue itself is a kind of moderation, a mean between extremes, and altogether results in the moderation of the excesses to which the individual might be prone. Virtue involves the chastening of the self at a certain level, the capacity to govern our tendency to act or desire in ways that are excessive. Moderation—while itself one of the virtues—might in fact be better understood to be virtue itself, inasmuch as all the particular virtues—such as courage, liberality, friendliness, modesty, and so on—are all themselves the result of moderation between excesses and deficiencies. And, when it comes to the virtue of moderation itself, Aristotle notes that it can be easily contrasted to its condition of excess, which he calls licentiousness or self-indulgence, but notes that one almost never finds its deficiency in nature, which he struggles to define and ultimately calls "insensibility." The ultimate human virtue—or perhaps, virtue itself—is achieved not by moderation, but by conquering the human propensity to seek its excess, "licentiousness." Moderation itself—the root of all the virtues—requires self-governance over our inclination to license.

For this reason, the central aim of education is to impart a kind of self-overcoming, and the sphere in which this is most comprehensively achieved is in the sphere of politics. Thus, for Aristotle, politics is itself a form of education, above all the education in self-governance (in all of its forms, individual and collective). Citizenship is defined as "ruling and being ruled in turn," the learned capacity to govern others and to be governed. The training in citizenship Aristotle compares to the training one would then, and still today, receive in the military:

> For this is what we speak of as political rule, and the ruler learns it by being ruled—just as the cavalry commander learns by being commanded, the general by being led, and [similarly in the case of] the leader of a regiment or company. Hence this too has been rightly said—that it is not possible to rule well without having been ruled.[1]

Governance of the self and society—and especially the appetites—requires a kind of training in the political sphere. That is to say, even as the citizenry is taught by the polity, the moderate citizenry is necessary to perpetuate a moderate regime. Thus, the moderate polity is relatively small, seeks not to engage in military activity for the sake of civic ag-

---

1 Aristotle, *Nicomachean Ethics*, Trans. Joe Sachs (Indianapolis, IN: Focus Books, 2002), III.4.

grandizement, and is moderate in its collective appetites. The city, in turn, must seek to moderate the tendency of economics to stray outside of its bounds, and in particular, to chasten the tendency of "the art of money-making" to seek its ends without limit. Aristotle insists that there is indeed a limit to acquisition—as there are in all human arts—and that part of learning the art of self-government is to distinguish between what he calls "mere living" and "living well," or what we might call "wants" and "needs." A main Aristotelian virtue, then, is frugality, and part of the object of human education in virtue aimed at human flourishing is to learn the boundaries of acquisition and to chasten our propensity for greed and envy.

Thus, finally, for Aristotle, the city is a preeminent teacher of citizens, and for this reason, the laws are understood to be forms of instruction. Unlike Hobbes—who wrote that "where the law is silent, one is free," by which he understood the law to be a set of boundaries outside of which it is silent about how one should live—for Aristotle, the law seeks to shape us as human beings with an orientation to the Good, and thus is rarely if ever silent. Thus writes Aristotle at the conclusion of his *Ethics*, in which he points to the necessity to a turn to *Politics* to see fully how the complete education of the human individual can take place:

> Hence it is necessary to arrange for rearing and exercises by laws, since they will not be painful when they have become habitual. And no doubt it is not enough for people to hit upon the right rearing and discipline when they are young, but also afterward, when they have reached adulthood, they must practice these things and habituate themselves, and we would need laws about these things as well, and so, generally, about the whole of life.[2]

What we need to note is that Politics is not preeminently the place of "policy," but of the aspiration to form good human character in accordance with human nature; but, that Politics finally cannot do this without first being composed of people of good character and formation. An ob-

---

2   Aristotle, *Nicomachean Ethics*, X.9.

vious circularity lies at the heart of Aristotle's arguments here, and it's one that's both unavoidable and salutary, because it cautions us against the view that absent an already well-formed citizenry, politics can be the realm of redemption—but also cautions us from the view that politics ought not to play any role in the formation of the character of citizens. We see the remnants of Aristotle's thought today on the Left in its call for a moral approach to the Economy and on the Right in its call for "Family Values," but these are both finally remnants of a broader and more comprehensive teaching about the human good that it would be first necessary to recover before we know what exactly would be worthy of conservation, that concept at the heart of "conservatism."

2. The Naturalness of Culture

Aristotle, then, clearly points to the need for a healthy and vibrant sphere that we would today call "culture." His emphasis upon education, the mutually reinforcing role of family and the broader society on the formation of the virtuous individual and polity, and the need for the resources of memory and history for the purposes of hitting the mark of moderation (thus, the central role of *phronesis*, or judgment) all point to the central role of *culture* in the formation of the flourishing human being. But, it was the late-seventeenth to mid-eighteenth-century thinker Giambattista Vico who first articulated a strong and forthright defense of culture in response to rising philosophies that were aimed at their evisceration. In particular, he saw in the philosophies of Descartes and Hobbes an articulation of human beings and human nature that reduced humans to utility-maximizing, instrumental rationalizers who were to make their self-maximizing calculations shorn of the inheritances of culture, history, place, tradition, and ancestry. The Cartesian and Hobbesian methodology posited that humans were best understood as rational calculators who made self-maximizing decisions in a condition of psychic isolation and radical autonomy. In order to most perfectly render those decisions, it was necessary theoretically to conceive of humans in a condition absent history, culture, community and memory, instead focusing solely on the knowable motivations within the isolated human heart (above all, according to Hobbes, desire and fear). Culture and history were understood to be accidental accretions, necessary to slough off in order to truly know our condition as humans. In turn, the science and politics of these thinkers was antithetical to culture, seeing its collection of practices, traditions and stories to be deceptive and misleading: modern science and liberal political theory proved to be the sledgehammers that destroyed culture wherever it was confronted.

Vico called this "a moral philosophy of solitaries." Instead, he argued that culture was "natural" to humans; indeed, that humans could not be conceived separate from or apart from culture. In response to Hobbes's theory of the State of Nature, Vico told a different story of the human past, in which humans did not become human until they became cultural beings. Focused especially on worship (the "cult" in culture, after all), marriage (along with childrearing within conjugal relations), and burial as constitutive elements of culture, Vico argued that it was when pre-human creatures began to settle into communities in which practices relating to worship, marriage, childrearing, and burial coalesced into the fabric of a culture, that the biological animal human became the moral creature human.

The wisdom of humans, then, was to be found not in abstractions or individuals apart from human society, but embedded within human communities. Vico argued against the abstract logic of Cartesians by asserting instead the primacy of what he called *"sensus communis,"* the sense of the community as the storehouse of wisdom, particularly manifested in culture, tradition, and memory. He argued that it was the shared "communal sense" of people within cultures that provided true guidance about right and wrong, about the proper and improper ways in which to act. He wrote that "human choice, by its nature most uncertain, is made certain and determined by the common sense of men with respect to human needs or utilities, [and is] the source of the natural law. Common sense is judgment without reflection, shared by an entire class of people, an entire nation, or the entire human race."[3]

Law and norms—even knowledge of the natural law—percolates up from the beliefs, behaviors, and activities of a community of people. In

3   Giambattista Vico, *The New Science of Giambattista Vico,* trans. Thomas Goddard Bergin and Max Harold Fisch, Third Edition (Ithaca, NY: Cornell University Press, 1984), 141–42.

contrast to a Kantian conception of law and ethics based upon abstractly-derived and universal criteria, for Vico (following Aristotle), law and ethics are ultimately *social*, embedded in practices, customs and traditions. The work of law thus is not abstracted from or even antithetical to the life of the community, but necessarily derives from it and requires intimate knowledge of the life of the community from which law arises. Alasdair MacIntyre echoes Vico when he argues that ethical judgments develop within traditions, and—by extension—that moral and ethical principles that find their formal expression in the law are derived from and bounded within that tradition.

Reflection upon the law, and its application to particular cases depends upon deep interpretive interrelationship between circumstance and principle, embedded within the deep knowledge of one's tradition. The practice and learning of law therefore involves "jurisprudence"— the linking of justice and prudence—knowledge of which derives from an extensive training in and familiarity with one's own tradition and culture. The law is thus to be considered as "a system of wisdom" that continues to accrue authority as new situations and experience are accumulated. The law is a "common inheritance," and hence is not solely the responsibility of the lawyerly class—though they certainly have a central role to play—but the people at large. Underlying the tradition of trial by jury is the belief that in the "sense of the community" the underlying wisdom and commonality of the law could be derived and affirmed.

If the broader populace is in some senses to know and live the law— at the very least, through the auspice of the culture itself—then the class of citizens devoted to working in and upon law must be broadly and liberally educated. An education in the law involves deep familiarity with the culture itself, as well as those classic elements of a liberal education, including especially those repositories of memory—history and the tradition of a culture, including all the belles letters (such as poetry, literature, and the fine arts)—as well as rhetoric and eloquence, the verbal bridge between individuals that calls upon a common storehouse of ideas, memories and stories. Knowledge of the law was akin less to a science than to an art. The lawyer was understood to be the very paragon of the liberally educated individual, the caretaker and conveyor of the culture in the form of the law, the intermediary between the "judgment without reflection" of the "sensus communis" and reflective judgment arising from prudence.

3. Thinking Generationally

This understanding of the centrality of culture and tradition in guiding human life and communities of course deeply informed the thought of Edmund Burke, who was responding to a radicalism of a different sort, the political radicalism of the French Revolution. Similarly based upon abstractions, the Revolutionaries attempted to impose a blueprint of an imagined world upon the messiness of human reality, with the expected Procrustean result of cutting off the heads of those who did not fit into the newer and better future. Burke famously articulated a stirring defense of tradition as a storehouse of memory, wisdom, and guidance, and urged that in the effort to correct some imperfections within traditions, modern "geometric" approaches to politics concluded that tradition itself needed to be eviscerated. Burke urged caution, circumspection, an acknowledgement of imperfection in all human affairs, and the patience of one whose political creed must echo that of the Hippocratic oath, "first do no harm."

In a famous passage in his *Reflections on the Revolution in France*, Burke sought to redefine the understanding of social contract theory that had gained prominence through the philosophical contributions of Thomas Hobbes and John Locke. That theory—based upon the anthropology of autonomous and radically individuated selves criticized by Vico—held that society was the result of a contract of self-interested selves who form political society for the sake of mutual advantage. Burke regarded this as a monstrous argument, one that underlay the radicalism of the French Revolution and its tendency to reject the relevance of the past in thinking about a perfected future. In effect, modern social contract theory destroyed the full spectrum of temporality, the continuity and connection between past, present and future. It premised that society was based upon the calculation of radically presentist selves, and thus that society could be remade at the whim of these ahistorical creatures. He intimated that such a philosophy led to a narrow utilitarian view of the world, in which necessarily radically individuated selves would pursue their interest with little regard for temporal consequences.

In response, Burke acknowledged that "society is indeed a contract," but of a specific kind. He argued that it was not a contract comparable to that of a commercial sort; rather, it is "to be looked on with other reverence, because it is not a partnership in things subservient only to the gross animal existence of a temporary and perishable nature. It is [rather] a partnership of all science; a partnership in all art; a partnership in every virtue and in all perfection. As the ends of such a partnership cannot be obtained in many generations, it becomes a partnership not only between those who are living, but between those who are living, those who are dead, and those who are to be born."[4] Human society is not a contract of specific interested parties striking a balance of interests for some narrow end, but rather a kind of process of sedimentation that goes on before we are born and continues after we die—or, to use another metaphor, a longstanding narrative in which we enter for a time, adding our stories, with the expectation that the narrative will continue and be further expanded after we die. How we interact with the world, its creatures, and our fellow humans is profoundly different depending on whether we view ourselves as part of a larger and more comprehensive fabric of generations, or more narrowly as mayflies that live for a day and die without knowledge of what has preceded or what will follow us.

Most obviously, Burke intends to promote a sense of reverence toward the inheritance of the past, and to advise against its radical alteration in ways contradictory to that inheritance. But of equal importance, if less noted, a central part of conservatism is due regard for the future, and for our obligations to generations not yet born. Our dispositions are to be simultaneously gratitude toward the past, but also a corresponding sense of obligation and responsibility toward the future. The two are connected: recognizing our debts to past generations, we seek to repay that debt through responsible stewardship for the sake of the unborn. The danger of the presentism of social contract theory is that it conceives of humans only acting within the context of their own generation, shorn of

4   Edmund Burke, *Reflections on the Revolution in France*, ed. J.G.A. Pocock (Indianapolis, IN: Hackett Publishing Company, Inc., 1987), 85.

past and future, and hence sets in motion a society not only that disregards the past, but discounts the future. The severing of the temporal dimension encourages a profound presentism, and attendant behavior that conserves little of the past and preserves little for the future.

This is a point made forcefully by among the most Burkean of contemporary philosophers, Roger Scruton, who spoke at Georgetown in 2007 on the theme of "Conservatism as Conservation." He noted that contemporary economic arrangements—ones that are often called "conservative"—provide a powerful incentive toward the "externalization of costs," the reduction of costs and activities that are typically transferred, if possible, to future generations. According to Scruton, it is conservatism's capacity to think not merely about the past, but to draw the future equally into the present, especially through a strong sense of the interconnection of gratitude and obligation among generations:

> So what is to stop us from externalizing our costs onto future generations? Within our own families, we recoil from doing such a thing. I don't want to dump the costs of my life on my son, even though I shall be dead when he feels them. Nor would I wish my grandchildren to pay the price of my selfishness.
>
> Through the device of the trust, English and American law has been able to protect the interests of absent generations by compelling the current owners of property to set their own interests aside. The trustees of a bequest must respect the wishes of the testator and in so doing—by holding their own desires and present emergencies in abeyance—will serve the interests of future generations. This form of ownership, and the moral idea contained in it, ought to be regarded as defining the conservative approach. We don't solve environmental problems by abandoning our attachment to private property or free enterprise, but we can make sure that these notions are shaped by the spirit of trusteeship.[5]

5   Roger Scruton, "A Righter Shade of Green," *American Conservative*: June 16, 2007.

By extension, law itself is to be understood as a kind of trust, the inheritance of the past intended to guide and inform the activities of the present with a view to our obligations to the future. Law is the codification of full temporality, an institution that connects the present to the past and the future. Law is not only normative—in Aristotle's sense—but it is broadly educative about our generational debts and obligations. At its best, the law is a tangible inheritance of the past, and one that each of us—above all those trained in the law—are obligated to regard with the responsibilities of trusteeship. It is itself an education in the full dimension of human temporality, meant to abridge our tendencies or temptations to live within the present, with the attendant dispositions of ingratitude and irresponsibility that such a narrowing of temporality encourages. Like other great human inheritances—our arts, our literature, our music, our architecture, our history, our religion—the law expands the human experience of time itself, making both the past and the future present to creatures that otherwise experience every moment solely in the present.

4. The Need for Formality and Forms

Tocqueville echoed Burke's concerns that modern democracy would be marked above all by a tendency toward "presentism." In its egalitarianism and especially its rejection of aristocracy, it would be suspicious of the past and the future, encouraging instead a kind of stunted individualism. Aristocracy, he wrote, "links everybody, from peasant to king, in one long chain. Democracy breaks the chain and frees each link . . . . Thus, not only does democracy make men forget their ancestors, but also clouds their view of their descendants and isolates them from their contemporaries. Each man is forever thrown back upon himself alone and there is a danger that he will be shut up in the solitude of his own heart."[6]

Tocqueville shared Burke's suspicion that modern democrats would be inclined to pursue things of the world with a kind of breathless abandon—no longer having a fixed place in the world as they did in aristocratic

6   Alexis de Tocqueville, *Democracy in America*, trans. George Lawrence (New York: Harper Perennial Modern Classics, 2000), II.ii.ii, 508.

times, denizens of liberal democracies would be noteworthy for their "restlessness," their constant striving for position and place in the wide-open competitive market where one could rapidly rise, and just as rapidly fall. This pursuit would further induce short-term thinking, and encourage a national disposition to individual materialism and pleasure-seeking.

In a remarkable passage (if one not often noted enough by even admirers of Tocqueville), Tocqueville argued that it is "forms" and "formalities" that democracies desperately need, but which they are likely inclined to reject out of hand.

> Men living in democratic centuries do not readily understand the importance of formalities and have an instinctive contempt for them . . . . Formalities arouse their disdain and even hatred. As they usually aspire to none but facile and immediate pleasures, they rush straight at the object of any of their desires, and the slightest delay exasperates them. This temperament, which they carry with them into political life, makes them impatient of the formalities which daily hold up or prevent one or another of their designs.[7]

Tocqueville draws upon earlier analysis in which he observes that a regime based in the idea of *equality* will make men bridle against the kinds of barriers and limits that forms and formalities represent. Forms are—as the word suggests—things of a defined shape, indicating what is contained within and what is outside, and thus prove to be offensive to the deeply democratic and egalitarian sensibilities of democrats. Thus, Tocqueville argues, so too are the very grounds for the forms, which is to inculcate a cultivation in self-control and restraint of appetite. This, too, becomes unbearable for the democrat.

Tocqueville would not be surprised at the decimation of forms in much of contemporary American life, from the mundane to comprehensive. Everyday dress reflects our society-wide devotion to informality (as we see institutionalized today in "Dress-down Fridays"). The use of honorific titles—such as Mr. or Mrs.—have increasingly dropped from

7   Tocqueville, *Democracy in America*, II.iv.7, 698.

our vocabularies. Etiquette is seen as a quaint if stuffy throwback that has been largely dispensed with (this fact was hilariously mocked in a Seinfeld episode in which the British aristocrat, Mr. Pitt, is seen eating a Snickers bar with a fork and knife). America's contribution to culinary art has largely been to take every food of the world and make it edible with one's hands and, if possible, in a shape that can be easily and quickly consumed in an automobile. In our universities, we have largely eliminated formal curricular requirements, replacing them with "distribution requirements" or altogether eliminating such requirements in order to offer a smorgasbord of choices for our students. We have largely dispensed with formal rules and behaviors of courtship, and have seen in its wake the rise of a "hook-up" culture. The nature and definition of "family" has become regarded as too limiting, and either it is to be whatever people want it to be, or it is to be eliminated in favor of informal relationships. And, perhaps the most remarkable sign of our informality is to be discerned in the frequent statement, especially among young people, that they are "spiritual, not religious." By this, it can only be meant that an amorphous and psychically comforting spirituality is what can be gleaned from the detritus of discarded theology, strictures, rituals, traditions and formalisms that have almost always defined religion (which comes from the Latin word *religare*, "to bind").

One sees the impatience of which Tocqueville writes in longstanding efforts to transform the Constitution from a formal structure that limits government, to one that empowers government to, in turn, increase individual liberty and even license. Contemporary jurisprudence has been the studied effort to deconstruct the formalism of the Constitution, and to replace it with a flexible and even infinitely elastic set of phrases that can be interpreted according to contemporary fashions. The theory of the "living Constitution" and "evolving standards" reflects this impatience with the formalism of the Constitution, and the unwillingness of its proponents to seek remedy through the formal process of constitutional amendment shows the impatience and even recklessness that Tocqueville wrote would mark the disposition of the modern democrat.

Ironically, it was the law—and perhaps above all lawyers—that Tocqueville believed would be repositories and defenders of forms and formalisms in a democratic age. Tocqueville wrote,

Men who have made special study of the laws and have derived therefrom habits of order, something of a taste of formalities, and an instinctive love for a regular concatenation
of ideas are naturally strongly opposed to the revolutionary
spirit and to the ill-considered passions of democracy . . . .

When the American people let themselves get intoxicated
by their own passions or carried away by their ideas, the
lawyers apply an almost invisible brake which slows them
down and halts them. Their aristocratic inclinations are se-
cretly opposed to the instincts of democracy, their supersti-
tious respect for all that is old to its love of novelty, their
narrow views to its grandiose designs, their taste for formalities to its scorn for regulations, and their habit of advancing
slowly to its impetuosity.[8]

Those who studied law according to this older meaning constituted, he
wrote, the naturally "conservative" element of society, those who would
correct democracy's worst inclinations, excesses and proclivities, and
thus defend a necessary aristocratic countertendency in defending
"forms." While Tocqueville might be disappointed to discover that the
lawyerly class today is more likely to be the most hostile toward forms
and be in the vanguard of dissolving the formalism of the Constitution,
it is doubtful that he would be altogether surprised.

Conclusion

Let me finish then, by suggesting four corresponding conclusions that
arise from the themes that I've explored in these four thinkers, ones that
would lie at the heart of an appropriate conservative self-understanding.

1. The private, public and social realms must be mutually reinforcing
    in promoting and reinforcing the inculcation of virtue. This is best
    done in local settings, and subsidiarity should be strongly encour-
    aged.

8   Tocqueville, *Democracy in America,* I.ii.8, 264, 268–69

2. As would follow a theory of subsidiarity, conservatism is the natural home of "multiculturalism" and "diversity," but a true and respectful disposition toward the varieties of cultures in the world. Conservatism ought to resist the modernist urge toward homogenization and monoculture. Diversity is not to be understood as individual-based, but community-based.

3. Conservatism needs to foster a long-term view, and correspondingly needs to stress an education steeped in knowledge of, and appreciation for, the past. In an era when many of the incentives in education tend to reward the purported "creation of new knowledge," conservatism needs to be equally cautious about an unreserved embrace of scientistic and technologic thinking as it is toward various versions of post-modernism.

4. Conservatism needs to defend, where they still exist, aristocratic inheritances of the past, and to seek the creation of new forms where possible. Conservatism should be suspicious of the "meritocratic" assumptions of modern life, ones aimed at eliminating the remnants of aristocracy, and which correspondingly have little patience with forms and with formalities. Meritocracy, so called, rewards the embrace of placelessness, deracination, short-term thinking, a cultivated kind of irresponsibility, and a disposition toward a belief in "problem-solving." It is the new ideology of our time, and conservatives should be willing to criticize it.

In sum, these four conclusions—and there are more—while potentially capable of being supported by politics and policy, cannot and do not draw a fine line between politics and culture. Culture—having its deepest sources in "cult"—is the natural medium of the conservative, and only to the extent that politics and policy can reinforce a good culture should conservatives see politics as an appropriate venue of attainment.

As should be obvious, conservatism as I have defined it is and remains the opponent of liberalism—with its tendency toward centralization and its progressive assumptions—but, perhaps more discomfiting, it is deeply critical of much of what passes today under the banner of conservatism. What we today call conservatism is often more the result of an accident of history—the Cold War in particular—than inherent to the definition of conservatism. Conservatism needs to rediscover its conservative roots, and can do so only in a most conservative manner—by tracing back into the past its origins and reasons for coming into existence. Only by looking back will we be prepared to look forward, and to repair the broken fabric of time that a most unconservative age has bequeathed us.

In 2010 I was invited by students at the Florida State University Law School to offer a lecture on the nature of conservatism. I was told that they would especially appreciate a lecture grounded in philosophy and the humanities, which they told me were in short supply in their law school classes. I had little experience addressing law students, and the resulting lecture was an effort to appeal to an older notion of law, particularly the kind that Tocqueville believed would serve as a kind of conserving ballast in democratic societies.

Chapter 8
Is There a Conservative Tradition in America?

In the third chapter of Volume 1 of Alexis de Tocqueville's masterpiece, *Democracy in America*, Tocqueville made the following rather startling claim:

> I am astonished that ancient and modern writers have not attributed to estate laws a greater influence on the course of human affairs. These laws belong, it is true, to the civil order; but they ought to be placed at the head of all political institutions, for they have incredible influence on the social state of peoples, of which political laws are only the expression.[1]

Tocqueville observed that from simple but stark differences in estate laws in his native France and America one could see a host of profound social and political effects. In France, he observed, the law of primogeniture governed inheritance of property, whereas in America, there was an emphasis upon equal division of property among all children when passing from one generation to the next.

The effects of this one difference, he argued, were striking and comprehensive. In France, "the family spirit is in a way materialized in the land. The family represents the land, the land represents the family; it perpetuates its name, its origin, its glory, its power, its virtues. It is an imperishable witness of the past and a precious pledge of existence to come."[2] This conclusion was more than merely theoretical for

1   Alexis de Tocqueville, *Democracy in America*, trans. George Lawrence (New York: Harper Perennial Modern Classics, 2000), I.i.3.
2   Tocqueville, *Democracy in America*, I.i.3.

Tocqueville, whose full name reflected his membership in an aristocratic family whose identity was bound up in a place. He was *de* Tocqueville—of Tocqueville—not only indicating his familial lineage, but his place in the world, the estate of Tocqueville near Cherbourg in Normandy, France. For a person living in an aristocratic society—whether or not a member of the aristocracy—what we call today "identity" is simply family and place, neither a matter of choice. One is who and where one came from, as signified in parts of names like "de," "von," "O'," "Mc," "-son" and so forth. Similarly, one was also defined by what one *did*, also more often than not a result of inheritance of profession from one's parents, whether one was a Miller or Weaver or Smith or Taylor, and so on. For Tocqueville, inheritance laws in aristocratic societies ensured a fixed identity that derived primarily from family and land. One was born and raised and lived on land that was composed of the decayed bones and humus of one's ancestors, just as one's remains would one day be the planting soil of one's heirs. The land and family were one.

By contrast, democratic America's insistence upon equal division of property led to the tendency to disassociate family from place, and even the identity of individuals from their families. Tocqueville noticed that in America, one's profession, one's self-definition, one's very identity was more often the result one's own work—one's successes and one's failures. As a result, Tocqueville writes, the decline of the "spirit of family" in a democratic age—a "spirit" that so centrally animates life in an aristocratic age—gives rise to "individualism," and more often than not, the pursuit of individual status through the pursuit of comparative wealth. The equal partitioning of inheritances, Tocqueville wrote, led to an extraordinary and universal pursuit of wealth: "I do not know of a country where the love of money holds a larger place in the heart of man," he observed, a consequence of basic changes to inheritance law.

The resulting society in a democracy, Tocqueville wrote, is one that is marked by what he calls "restlessness." Because democratic peoples define who they are by means of their own exertions, America is marked by a constant and unceasing activity, propelled by the fear that if one is not rising, one is falling. But while this condition is one of extreme liberation to pursue whatever destiny one wishes, it is at the same time a source of profound and constant anxiety. "Restlessness" is captured in that suggestive phrase of our Declaration of Independence, the right to the "pursuit of happiness," with the plaintive suggestion that it is the pursuit that is available to us, and that happiness lies just out of reach. By contrast, aristocratic society is marked by "quietude," or our most direct translation of that word "quiescence"—acceptance, even resignation, but also firm knowledge of who one is, the solidity of one's identity and station.

There is a reason that *The Great Gatsby* remains for many the "Great American Novel." We both identify with, and are repulsed by, Jay Gatsby, who having—it seems—achieved all of his dreams, could nevertheless find no contentment. "He stretched out his arms toward the dark water in a curious way, and, far as I was from him, I could have sworn he was trembling. Involuntarily I glanced seaward—and distinguished nothing except a single green light, minute and far away . . . Gatsby believed in the green light, the orgiastic future that year by year recedes before us. It eluded us then, but that's no matter—to-morrow we will run faster, stretch out our arms farther . . . . And one fine morning . . ."

Gatsby's anxiety, captured by Tocqueville, remains ours, even seems to get worse year by year. This anxiety isn't just a character flaw of a fictional character, but begins to define who we are at a younger and younger age. Most students will recognize it as a defining feature of their time in high school, and doesn't cease once a promising student gets into the college of her dreams. This gnawing and ceaseless worry continues to define so much of the waking lives of students I've taught at places like Princeton, Georgetown and now Notre Dame. We live in the world described by Tocqueville, calling it the "meritocracy," which has the virtue of allowing us to define our own lives, our own trajectory, our own futures, but with the downside of a never-ending anxiety that we won't make it, someone will displace us, we will fall below where we started. Worse still, the goalpost constantly moves, so that once one has achieved one's goal and dreams—that thick envelope from the likes of Harvard, Princeton, Yale—one is entitled perhaps to a day or two of celebration, before once again one begins to fret about the right dorm, the right clubs, the right major, the right friends, the right internship, the right life.

I begin here to point out that what we typically regard as debates between conservatives and liberals don't begin to approach the differences that defined an aristocratic and democratic society in the form that

Tocqueville perceived. There are not many conservatives around today who argue that children should be defined by the name that they received from their parents, or that they should marry those who their parents arrange for them; not many who argue that one's horizon should be defined by the place where one was born and an economy that is relatively static; nor that rule should be lodged in those who have ruled in the past, by virtue of their birthright.

Today's conservatives are—well, they are liberals. They are a distinctive kind of liberal, with roots in the philosophy that was first developed as a rejection of the aristocratic world that Tocqueville saw passing out of existence even in his time. Today's conservatives are likely to appeal to the eternal verities of the Declaration of Independence and the Constitution and the wisdom of America's Founders. The philosophy that animated the Founding Fathers was the philosophy of figures like Thomas Hobbes and John Locke, both of whom argued that humans were by nature free and independent, and imagined a condition that existed before the establishment of society, of culture, of laws and civilization. This, they argued, was man's "natural condition," a state of nature in which humans were imagined as radically autonomous selves, defined by independence, not relationships, by freedom, not obligations. They argued that society only came into existence when these individuals agreed by free consent, through a "social contract," that they would put themselves under a common authority whose main purpose was to "secure their rights." Government and human society comes into existence in order to protect our rights to individual autonomy.

This philosophy undergirded the kind of liberation from tradition, from place, from generational definition that Tocqueville saw as the hallmark of an aristocratic age. It allowed especially for the explosion of individual innovation and energy that has been one of the hallmarks of American society—a result of the "restlessness" that Tocqueville observed. But it also led to an extreme weakening of traditional forms of belonging and membership, of deep ties that people might have as a result of longstanding relationships that develop in particular places across many generations. It also led to even more extreme forms of inequality than had existed in an aristocratic age, the particular kind of inequality that a dynamic economy can generate.

The outcomes of this original—or classical—liberalism gave rise to a reaction in the late nineteenth and twentieth centuries, the rise of progressive liberalism. Progressive liberalism—developed by thinkers such as John Dewey and Herbert Croly, and advanced by political figures like Woodrow Wilson and Theodore Roosevelt and later Franklin Roosevelt—was especially critical of the deep-seated individualism at the heart of the classical liberal tradition. It called for the development of a national form of fellow feeling, a recognition of shared fates that what Dewey called "the old individualism" could not adequately recognize. Figures like Dewey and Croly in particular called for a strengthening and expansion of the national government as a locus of our shared fates, the entity that could at once both help equalize the titanic inequalities of the Progressive era, as well as serve as a new locus of membership, identity, and even—in the words of Croly—the basis of "the brotherhood of man."

In a nutshell, the ongoing debate between what we call "conservatives" and "liberals" in America remains defined by this division within liberalism—between classical liberals and progressive liberals. We call the first "conservatives" because they are the heirs of the older liberal tradition within America, and hence, seek to "conserve" the principles of the American founding against efforts to change the nature of the American polity. The second have come to prefer the label "progressive," indicating their connection to the Progressive tradition and its attraction to equality and overcoming individualism, but it's fair to say that both versions of liberalism are equally supportive of "progress" and hostile to the traditionalism of aristocratic society. Both these major camps in our contemporary politics are heirs of the liberal tradition. Both parties support a dynamic and rapidly changing society. Today's conservatives mainly seek this liberal end through support of a highly deregulated market economy whose hallmark is what the political economist Joseph Schumpeter called "creative destruction." The figure who is widely regarded as the greatest conservative political figure of the twentieth century—Ronald Reagan—was fond of quoting Thomas Paine, and especially a phrase from Paine's pamphlet "Common Sense" in which Paine declared "I believe that we have it in our power to make the world over again." Paine was to become the great intellectual opponent of the political philosopher Edmund Burke—the founder of conservatism. Revealingly, Ronald Reagan was far more likely to quote Paine than Burke.

For all of their differences, the two liberalisms that comprise our political horizon—"conservative" liberalism and "progressive" liberalism—share certain fundamental features in common. First, they are both born of deep hostility toward old aristocracy. Both seek to replace the old aristocracy with a new meritocracy. If today's progressives are more likely to be concerned about the inequalities generated by our ever-more-perfect meritocracy, they are nevertheless not calling for its elimination. Few progressives that I know are likely, for instance, to call for the replacement of the current practice of college admissions with admissions by lottery (a much more radical egalitarian approach, after all). Let's face it—among the main winners in today's meritocracy are Progressive liberals. They seek to reduce the inequalities that are one of its main effects, a concern born to significant extent from their very success in having navigated its currents.

Both classical liberalism and progressive liberalism are born of a deep mistrust toward the past—which is viewed as a source of unchosen authority, a potential limitation upon freedom, and a shackle upon a dynamic and rapidly changing society. Both are equally animated by a pervasive suspicion of unchosen bonds and relationships, agreeing that a central feature of personal liberty and independence rests on our right as individuals to make and revise any and all relationships. Both have a deep mistrust toward "constitutive" organizations that are not fully chosen—from marriage to one's immediate neighborhood to one's friends, colleagues, one's religion (or irreligion), any club, organization, association. Progressive liberalism began by suggesting that the membership that ought to define us is our membership in the comprehensive national attachment (the "New Republic," the title of the journal founded by John Dewey and Herbert Croly). In an interesting twist, that identity to nation is more likely to be embraced today by "classical liberals," while "progressive liberals" have moved increasingly to urge us to recognize our membership more broadly in a global community. Both commend memberships based upon relatively abstract bonds, ones that have to be imagined rather than the result of deep personal engagement.

What I'm suggesting is that liberalism is, in its core commitments, not a political philosophy that seeks to "conserve"; rather, it seeks to generate new possibilities, new vistas, new opportunities by liberating people from what had been traditional forms of membership of the type described by Tocqueville—that "family spirit" that animated a sense of deep belonging in a place, with a people, in a long chain of generations. Classical liberalism sought to free people of thick forms of identity that were inherited from past generations and necessarily bound up with the fate of others; progressive liberalism sought to infuse a sense of common fate to a world of individuals created by classical liberalism, but a thin sense of belonging to a vast "community" whose agent would increasingly be a distant government that would ask little of us personally. The measure of our difference would increasingly come down to debates over tax rates and levels of economic regulation, while sharing a more fundamental commitment to a society defined by dynamism, individual liberty, freedom from the past and a shared commitment to progress.

In fact, Tocqueville discerned a deep connection between these two camps, between a society that would be founded on a central commitment to individualism and a reaction that would posit that the solution to individualism lie in the empowering of a central, national government. In the last chapters of *Democracy in America*, Tocqueville wrote of his fears of the rise of something he called "Democratic Despotism," a wholly new kind of government that the world had never encountered before. This was not the classical form of despotism, in which a dictatorial power sought the brutal enslavement of a captive population, but rather a "soft" despotism in which a citizenry invited and desired the care of a "tutelary state." Tocqueville prophesized that a society defined by constantly restless and anxious individuals would discover that they had no firm bonds on which to rely, no deep commitments to which they could turn in times of trial and trouble. In an advanced democratic age, he wrote, one could expect that a society of radically individuated selves would have nowhere to turn but the State.

> "I want to imagine under what new features despotism could present itself to the world; I see an innumerable crowd of similar and equal men who spin around restlessly, in order to gain

small and vulgar pleasures with which they fill their souls. Each one of them, withdrawn apart, is like a stranger to the destiny of all the others; his children and his particular friends form for him the entire human species; as for the remainder of his fellow citizens, he is next to them, but he does not see them; he touches them without feeling them; he exists only in himself and for himself alone . . . .

Above those men arises an immense and tutelary power that alone takes charge of assuring their enjoyment and of looking after their fate. It is absolute, detailed, regular, far-sighted, and mild. It would resemble paternal power if, like it, it had as a goal to prepare men for manhood; but on the contrary it seeks only to fix them irrevocably in childhood; it likes the citizens to enjoy themselves. It works willingly for their happiness; but it wants them to be the unique agent for it and the sole arbiter; it attends to their security, provides for their needs, facilitates their pleasures, conducts their principled affairs, directs their industry, settles their estates, divides their inheritances; how can it not remove entirely from them the trouble to think and the difficulty of living? This is how it makes the use of free will less useful and rarer every day; how it encloses the action of the will within a smaller space and little by little steals from each citizen even the use of himself."[3]

This is a passage in Tocqueville that has always been embraced and lauded by American conservatives, but what they generally fail to notice is that the rise of the central "tutelary power" is not the result of a "collectivist" impulse, but the very forms of individualism that classical liberalism assumes to be at the core of human nature. What we tend to regard as a great and yawning divide between the philosophies of American conservatives and liberals—between classical liberals and progressive conservatives—is, by Tocqueville's telling, in fact a deeply interconnected relationship. Having dispelled the thick set of ties that

3   Tocqueville, *Democracy in America*, II.iv.6.

define aristocratic society, classical liberalism gives rise to the solution demanded by progressive liberalism. Rather than polar opposites, they are different sides of the same coin.

Tocqueville fears this possible fate of democracy. Throughout his long text analyzing the triumph of democracy in America, and eventually throughout the world, he simultaneously acknowledges the benefits of a society that frees people from the unjust limitations of aristocratic society while lamenting as well for some of what is likely to be lost. In the very first pages of "Democracy in America" he states that he writes his book in order to "tutor" democracy, to tame its worst instincts and perhaps above all to help it avoid the fate of democracy becoming too much itself.

What Tocqueville commends above is the effort to retain certain inheritances or even functional analogues of the fading aristocratic age as leaven against democracy's tendency to undermine itself. These involve the effort to "conserve" the central importance of memory; a sense of connection between the past, the present and the future; and the responsibility and accountability that comes from a sense of rootedness, all of which are distinctive features of the aristocratic age, against the spirit of restlessness, individualism and accompanying sense of civic helplessness of the democratic age. Foremost among these inheritances were three that had aristocratic origins: first, a strong role for law and members of the legal profession as the heirs of "common law," or tradition as it is passed through the accumulation of cases and judgments; second, a rich tapestry of associational life, local institutions that brought people together and fostered identities both broader than democratic individualism yet more local and diverse than liberal statism; and third, religion as a rock and anchor in an often tumultuous democratic age.

A preeminent legacy that needs conserving is an older understanding of liberty that can come to stand at odds with the liberal definition of liberty. Early in *Democracy in America*, Tocqueville contrasted the classical definition of liberty as the art of self-rule, with the liberal definition of liberty being the ability to do as one wishes. Tocqueville writes with admiration for the Puritan roots of the local democratic practices of New England townships, which are animated by the direct engagement in political rule by the citizens of those local townships.

He called these the "schools of democracy," a place where one learns the "discipline of freedom," particularly the art of making laws that will in turn govern us. This practice was deepened by what he recommended were the "arts of association," the engagement of people in various civic and political groups that had the power, he argued, to "enlarge the heart." His great fear of "democratic despotism" was his worry that a democracy animated by a definition of liberty to do as one likes would ironically be an abandonment of the practices of democratic self-governance. Recent findings from social science has consistently confirmed Tocqueville's fears, showing consistent declines of participation in a wide variety of associations. As dramatically described in a 1995 article by political scientist Robert Putnam, Americans are bowling as much as ever, but fewer of those are bowling in leagues. Instead, they are "bowling alone."[4]

Second, he worried that a society driven by restless ambition for self-definition, centered around the pursuit of money, would become solely oriented toward utilitarianism. He foresaw a decline of interest in the tradition of the liberal arts, in an engagement with what we would call the humanities, and a declining interest in beauty and leisure in favor of that which was useful, practical, and temporary. Speaking of the future-orientation of Americans—driven by their restlessness and sense of having been liberated from the past—he observed that their belief in progress and even "perfectibility" led them to make shoddy work in the present, believing that future inventions and developments would make current investments and efforts irrelevant. Recent trends in higher education suggest his worries were again justified, as we see widespread declines in liberal arts and humanities as fields of study, and a corresponding rise in the study of business and other "practical" kinds of disciplines, none of which lay claim to teaching the arts of thinking, speaking and reading and that have historically been closely linked to the practices of free citizenship.

Third and finally, he worried about the narrowing of temporal horizons for democratic humanity, focused mainly on current gratification,

---

4   Robert Putnam, *Bowling Alone: The Collapse and Revival of American Community* (New York: Simon & Schuster, 2001).

counting on the future to solve any resulting problems, and generally dismissive toward the past. He noted that an aristocratic age encouraged the sense that a present generation owed debts to past generations, and as a result, generated obligations to future generations. By contrast, denizens of a liberal age would be more likely to feel released from obligations, and instead generate debt for future generations. Only a lengthened time horizon would make it more likely that we would experience ourselves as something more than self-created individuals, but as members in a chain of relationships, and thereby aspire to contribute to a common deposit that had been built by those who long preceded us, and those who would follow us. Today we see growing concerns about the costs of our pervasive "presentism," with those on the Right lamenting the increase of federal debt while those on the Left warn of the accumulating costs of environmental degradation. What they tend to have in common is their recognition that the costs of truly addressing each problem are so steep that our political order is not very likely to successfully call upon the necessary sacrifices of those who have grown comfortable by living in the present.

While I disavowed the seemingly inaccurate title of this talk at the beginning of my lecture, perhaps after all it's true—it's hard to be a conservative in America, because it's not built into the fabric of the American political tradition to conserve, but to spend; to waste, not to save; to face forward, not look back. And while an observer like Tocqueville would be the first to acknowledge all that is gained by this transformation, he would also remind us of its costs—something that it's difficult for us to see, lacking, as we do, a conservative tradition in America.

This chapter was the result of an invitation to deliver the 2015 Hemmeter Lecture at the Montclair Kimberley Academy, a private high school, in Montclair, New Jersey. This endowed lecture aims to bring a visible thinker to discuss crucial political and social issues of the day, and I was told by the organizers that I had been invited in order to hear from someone of a conservative disposition that was otherwise a largely unknown species in those precincts. For that occasion I decided that rather than defend what generally passed for conservatism, I would stipulate that the thing they generally thought of as conservatism was severely wanting. However, rather than suggest that the alternative was standard-issue liberalism, I recommended instead an approach that could be properly conceived as conservative, but which was not advanced by any particular party in the current American political landscape. The presentation was well-received, both to my surprise, and I think that of my audience.

Part 3
American Dusk?

Chapter 9
Community and Liberty
OR Individualism and Statism

Two narratives today dominate our political landscape, both of which claim to protect the cherished value of Liberty against unjust political encroachments and limits. One, from conservatives, poses liberty in the form of individual rights—especially of property—against the collectivism of "progressive" liberalism or Statism. The other, from progressives, opposes limits on personal liberty - especially in the area of sexual autonomy - against a paternalistic state.

One might reasonably conclude that, for Americans, liberty's reign is inviolate, even if its definition is deeply contested. In spite of disagreements, it seems widely agreed upon that liberty is the condition that exists when state limitation is absent. Thus, if we confine ourselves to this predominant understanding of liberty, the two sides share a fundamental starting point. But such a starting point also suggests that Americans speak of liberty in a severely limited language, even one that finally leads to an incomplete and even mistaken set of conclusions about the relationship between Liberty and the State, as well as individualism and collectivism. I want to suggest a better starting point is needed.

By expanding our consideration to a different understanding of liberty, we change our position somewhat and see with more clarity that, what looks from our current position like a deep antipathy between individualism and Statism, is in point of fact something more of a continuity and logical progression. Without the addition of a distinct understanding of liberty to that of classical liberalism, from close up, all that we can discern are the opposite features of the two dominant political views of our day. By expanding our vista, however, we can better discern their relatedness, and propose that a true alternative is not be-tween these siblings, but between a false choice of these two ideologies and a true choice between distinct and competing ideas of the very nature of liberty itself.

While there are a number of thinkers who can aid us in this expansion of our vocabulary, one thinker I wish today to highlight is one of the most penetrating and prescient of the mid-twentieth-century con-servative authors, the sociologist Robert Nisbet. I will have recourse to some of his powerful insights in his 1953 book *The Quest for Commu-nity*—recently re-issued by ISI Books—as well as his later 1975 book *Twilight of Authority*. Nisbet's key insight, variously articulated, was that Statism is a logical and even inevitable consequence of individ-ualism—and thus, that the apparently opposite and conflicting philoso-phies of classical liberalism and progressive liberalism are actually inseparable. If this is the case, to seek to combat iterations of collectivism by appeal to the individualistic principles of classical liberalism is to be engaged in the philosophical equivalent of throwing gasoline on a fire.

At the heart of Nisbet's analysis is the following claim—human be-ings are by nature social and relational creatures, and that modern liber-alism begins with a set of assumptions that contradict that reality. In so doing, the assumption of anthropological individualism at the heart of liberalism, and the practical realization of individualism in the world, deforms the human person. It is this deformation—particularly the evis-ceration of a thick set of identities embedded in a variety of groups, whether family, community, polity, church, or any other of other institu-tions and organizations—that fosters the conditions that makes collec-tivism an attractive and even inevitable alternative. Without the rise of individualism, the rise of collectivism is inconceivable. To take recourse to an important image from an essay by Leo Strauss, the two philoso-phies represent major "waves" of modern thought—and, like waves, one forms from the material that preceded it onto the shore.

Before exploring this dynamic in more detail, let me first contrast two competing understandings of liberty, one largely developed in the ancient and Christian world, and the other centrally developed in the early-modern period by, among others, the philosopher John Locke. Both claim the "language of liberty," but if one is true, the other is false, but, importantly too, it is only from the perspective of ancient liberty that one can see more clearly the close relationship between the individualism of classical liberalism and the collectivism of progressive liberalism.

Modern liberalism begins not—as might be believed if we were to follow the narrative of contemporary discourse—in opposition to Statism or Progressivism, but rather in explicit and intense rejection of ancient political thought and especially its basic anthropological assumptions. Hobbes, among others, is frequently explicit in his criticisms of both Aristotle and "the Scholastics"—that Catholic philosophy particularly influenced by Thomas Aquinas, who was of course particularly influenced by Aristotle. Modern liberal theory thus began with an explicit rejection of Aristotelian/Thomist anthropology. According to Aristotle, and later further developed by Aquinas, man is by nature a social and political animal—which is to say, that humans only become human in the context of polities and society. Shorn of such relations, the biological creature "human" was not actually a fully realized human—not able to achieve the telos of the human creature, a telos that required law and culture, cultivation and education, and hence, society and tradition. Thus, Aristotle was able to write (and Aquinas after him essentially repeated) that "the city is prior to the family and the individual"—not, of course, temporally, but in terms of the primacy of wholes to parts. To use a metaphor common to both the ancients and in the Biblical tradition, the body as a whole "precedes" in importance any of its constitutive parts: without the body, neither the hand, nor foot, nor any other part of the body is viable.

Within human societies, to the extent that humans are able to develop true and flourishing individuality, it is only by means of political society and its constitutive groups and associations, starting of course with the family. An essential component of our capacity to achieve human flourishing is our learned ability to place ourselves under rule and law. At first, as children, we are expected to obey because of the claims of authority—we follow rules and law because we are told to do so by our elders. As we grow in maturity and self-knowledge, we assume the responsibility of self-government—ideally in a form that is continuous between the individual and the city. For the ancients, liberty is the cultivated ability to exercise self-governance, to limit ourselves in accordance with our nature and the natural world.

The various practices by which we exercise self-limitation and self-governance is comprehensively called virtue. By contrast, for the ancients, the inability or unwillingness to exercise virtue was tantamount to the absence of liberty. The unbridled or even extensive pursuit of appetite led necessarily to a condition of servitude and even slavery—slavery to one's passions. Thus, for the ancients, law was not an unnatural imposition of humanity's natural freedom; rather, law (ideally, a self-imposed law) was the necessary and enabling condition for liberty.

This idea of liberty is certainly not unknown in more recent times, though it is rarely articulated. One can find it, for instance, beautifully stated in the second verse of Katherine Lee Bates's hymn "America the Beautiful":

> O beautiful for pilgrim feet
> Whose stern impassioned stress
> A thoroughfare of freedom beat
> Across the wilderness!
> America! America!
> God mend thine every flaw,
> Confirm thy soul in self-control,
> Thy liberty in law!

Most Americans today might not recognize the deep philosophical principle contained in the statement "liberty in law," linked to "self-control," but Bates was thinking precisely of the classical definition of liberty that was embraced wholesale by the Puritans (pilgrims), who transported it to the United States fundamentally intact, and which provoked Tocqueville's admiration of Puritan's "noble" definition of liberty at the outset of *Democracy in America*.[1]

The ancients emphasized the necessity of an appropriate scale in which such human flourishing could take place. First, the experience of law must necessarily be close, not distant, and must ideally be experienced as a form of self-governance. The more distant and impersonal

1   Alexis de Tocqueville, *Democracy in America*, trans. George Lawrence (New York: Harper Perennial Modern Classics, 2000), I.i.ii.

the promulgation of law, the more it would necessarily be experienced as an external and even unnatural imposition upon me, and a divide would open between law and liberty (government "out there"). Additionally, the larger the scale, the law would fall generally and categorically upon a variety of circumstances, thus tending to inherent injustice as the natural variety and distinctiveness of human arrangements would be ignored or dismissed. Further, a large scale also lent itself to the anonymity and corresponding forms of irresponsibility (think of nature of anonymous commentary on many websites), while undermining the kinds of trust and responsibility that were required to foster a sense of gratitude and corresponding obligation between generations. Another consideration was that large-scale political entities tended to aim at national or imperial greatness and wealth, and thus tended to stoke and tempt the appetites and undermine the inculcation of virtue. Ancient theory thus centrally considered the appropriate scale in which liberty as the practice of self-government through virtue could be realized. Liberty, so conceived, could only be realized in a small and local setting.

For the ancients, the highest aim of society was the flourishing of the free, self-governing individual and the achievement of our particular capacities—our talents and abilities—but such "individuality" could only be achieved through the auspices of our political and social relationships. Thus, even as we might flourish in our particular gifts, we are simultaneously obligated to acknowledge that such gifts have their source in and through the contributions of our community. The achievement of our full humanity is necessarily appropriately accompanied by a disposition of gratitude, and a corresponding assumption of obligation to proffer the same prospects for future generations. Thus, while classical philosophy—especially Aristotelian and Thomistic iterations—extolled the condition of achieving the condition of a free individual, it was a philosophy that could be confused as aiming at "individualism." The properly cultivated individual can never conceive of, much less experience, a wholly separate relationship to his community. It is incorrect to suppose that ancient thought denied a place for "liberty" or the aspiration to achieving distinct forms of individuality, but the context and definition of each differs considerably from contemporary understandings.

*** *** ***

Liberal theory fiercely attacked this fundamental assumption about human nature. Hobbes and Locke alike—for all their differences—begin by conceiving humans by nature not as parts of wholes, but as wholes apart. We are by nature "free and independent," naturally ungoverned and even non-relational. There is no ontological reality accorded to groups of any kind—as Bertrand de Jouvenel quipped about social contractarianism, it was a philosophy conceived by "childless men who had forgotten their childhoods." Liberty is a condition in which there is a complete absence of government and law, and "all is right"—that is, everything that can be willed by an individual can be done. Even if this condition is posited to show its unbearableness or untenability, the definition of natural liberty posited in the "state of nature" becomes a regulative ideal—liberty is ideally the ability of the agent to do whatever he likes. In contrast to ancient theory, liberty is the greatest possible pursuit and satisfaction of the appetites, while government is a conventional and unnatural limitation upon our natural liberty.

For both Hobbes and Locke, we enter into a social contract not only to secure our survival, but to make the exercise of our liberty more secure. Both Hobbes and Locke—but especially Locke—understand that liberty in our pre-political condition is limited not only by the lawless competition of other individuals, but by the limitations that a recalcitrant and hostile nature imposes upon us. A main goal of Locke's philosophy especially is actually to expand the prospects for our liberty—defined as the capacity to satisfy our appetites—now through the auspices of the State. We come to accept the terms of the social contract because its ultimate effect will actually increase our personal liberty by expanding the capacity of human control over the natural world. Locke writes that the law works to increase liberty, by which he means our liberation from the constraints imposed by the natural world.

Thus, for liberal theory, while the individual "creates" the State through the social contract, in a practical sense the liberal State "creates" the individual by providing the conditions for the expansion of liberty, now defined increasingly as the capacity of humans to expand their mastery over nature. Far from there being an inherent conflict between the individual and the State—as so much of modern political reporting would suggest—liberalism establishes a deep and profound connection between the liberal ideal of liberty that can only be realized through the auspices of a powerful State. The State does not merely serve as a referee between contesting individuals; in securing our capacity to engage in productive activities, especially commerce, the State establishes a condition in reality that existed in theory only in the State of Nature—that is, the ever-increasing achievement of the autonomous, freely choosing individual. Rather than the State acting as an impediment to the realization of our individuality, the State becomes the main agent of our liberation from the limiting conditions in which humans have historically found themselves.

Thus, one of the main roles of the liberal State becomes the active liberation of individuals from any existing limiting conditions. At the forefront of liberal theory is the liberation from limitations imposed by nature upon the achievement of our desires—one of the central aims of life, according to Locke, being the "indolency of the body." A main agent in that liberation becomes commerce, the expansion of opportunities and materials by which to realize not only existing desires, but even to create new ones that we did not yet know we had. One of its earliest functions is to support that basic role it assumes in extending the conquest of nature. The State becomes charged with extending and expanding the sphere of commerce, particularly enlarging the range of trade and production and mobility (e.g., the Constitution positively charges Congress to "promote the Progress of sciences and useful arts"—"Progressivism" is already in the Constitution). The expansion of markets and the attendant infrastructure necessary for that expansion is not, and cannot be, the result of "spontaneous order"; rather, an extensive and growing State structure is necessary to achieve that expansion, even at times to force recalcitrant or unwilling participants in that system into submission (see, for instance, J. S. Mill's recommendation in *Considerations on Representative Government* that the enslavement of "backward" peoples can be justified if they are forced to lead productive economic lives).

One of the main goals of the expansion of commerce is the liberation of otherwise embedded individuals from their traditional ties and relationships. The liberal State serves not only the "negative" (or

reactive) function of umpire and protector of individual liberty; simultaneously it also takes on a "positive" (that is to say, active) role of "liberating" individuals who, in the view of the liberal State, are prevented
from making the wholly free choices of liberal agents. At the heart of
liberalism is the supposition that the individual is the basic unit of
human existence, the only natural human entity that exists. If liberal
theory posits the existence of such individuals in an imaginary "state
of nature," liberal practice—beginning, but not limited to the rise of
commerce—seeks to expand the conditions for the realization of the
individual. The individual is to be liberated from all the partial and limiting affiliations that pre-existed the liberal State, if not by force (though
that may at times be necessary), then by constantly lowering the costs
and barriers to exit. The State lays claim to govern all groupings within
the society—it is the final arbiter of legitimate and illegitimate groupings, and from its point of view, the only ontological realities are the
individual and the State (for evidence of this fact, consider the fron-
tispiece of Hobbes's *Leviathan*). Eventually the State lays claim to set
up its own education system to ensure that children are not overly
shaped by family, religion or any particular community; through its
legal and police powers, it will occasionally force open "closed" communities as soon as one person claims some form of unjust assertion
of authority or limits upon individual freedom; it even regulates what
is regarded to be legitimate and illegitimate forms of religious worship.
Marriage is a bond that must be subject to its definition. A vast and intrusive centralized apparatus is established not to oppress the population, but rather to actively ensure the liberation of individuals from any
forms of constitutive groups or supra-individual identity. Thus, any organizations or groups or communities that lay claim to more substantive
allegiance will be subject to State sanctions and intervention (see for
instance, the efforts of the Obama administration to bring Belmont
Abbey College and other religious institutions to heel through such di-
rectives as the HHS mandate), but this oppression will be done in the
name of the liberation of the individual. Any allegiance to sub-national
groups, associations, or communities comes to be redefined not as inheritances, but as memberships of choice with very low if any costs to
exit. Modern liberals are to be pro-choice in every respect; one can

limits one's own autonomy, but only if one has chosen to do so, and generally only if one can revise one's choice at a later date—which means, in reality, one hasn't really limited one's autonomy at all. All choices are fungible, alterable, and reversible. The vow "til death do us part" is subtly but universally amended—and understood—to mean, "or until we choose otherwise."

*** *** ***

Various forms of Statism thus arise quite logically from these basic aspects of the liberal system. Progressive philosophy agrees fundamentally with the liberal vision of the liberation of the individual from all partial and mediating institutions, but eventually comes to include the State itself as one of those partial and limiting associations. This follows with iron and inevitable logic: if the State is the creation of individuals, then eventually the State itself needs to be abolished to achieve the thoroughgoing liberty of the individual from all partial associations. Marxism's dream of the "withering away of the State" is a logical extension of the trajectory of liberalism.

It is here that Robert Nisbet notices some additional relationships between the two. It is only when the variety of institutions and organizations of humankind's social life have been eviscerated—when the individual experiences himself as an individual—that collectivism as a theory becomes plausible as a politics in fact. Liberalism's successful liberation of individuals from what had historically been "their own" and the increasing realization of the "individual" made it possible for the theory of cosmopolitanism to arise as an actionable political program in the modern era. The idea that we could supersede all particular attachments and achieve a kind of "cosmic consciousness" or experience of our "species being" was a direct consequence of the lived experience of individualism. Locke is the midwife to Marx, in a manner of speaking.

Nisbet also notes the psychological conditions arising from liberalism's unfolding that also give rise to a longing for collectivism. He argued that collectivism arises as a reaction against the atomization of liberalism. The active dissolution of traditional human communities and institutions provokes a violent reaction in which a basic human need—

"the quest for community"—is no longer being met. As naturally "political" or "social" creatures, we long for a thick and rich set of constitutive bonds that necessarily shape a fully-formed human being. Shorn of the deepest ties to family (extended), place, community, region, religion, and culture—and deeply shaped to believe that these forms of association are limits upon our autonomy—we seek membership and belonging, and a form of extended self-definition, through the only legitimate form of organization available to liberal man—the State.

Nisbet saw the modern rise of Fascism and Communism as the predictable consequence of the early-modern liberal attack upon smaller associations and communities—shorn of those memberships, modern liberal man became susceptible to the quest for belonging now to distant and abstract State entities. In turn, those political entities offered a new form of belonging by adopting the evocations and imagery of those memberships that they had displaced, above all by offering a new form of quasi-religious membership, now in the Church of the State itself. Our "community" was now to be a membership of countless fellow humans who held in common an abstract allegiance to a political entity that would assuage all of our loneliness, alienation, and isolation. It would provide for our wants and needs; all that was asked in return was sole allegiance to the State, and the partial or even complete elimination of any allegiance to any other intermediary entity. To provide for a mass public, more power to the central authority was asked and granted. Thus Nisbet concludes, following a basic insight of Alexis de Tocqueville: "It is impossible to understand the massive concentrations of political power in the twentieth century, appearing so paradoxically, or it has seemed, right after a century and a half of individualism in economics and morals, unless we see the close relationship that prevailed all through the nineteenth century between individualism and State power and between both of these together and the general weakening of the area of association that lies intermediate to man and the State."

Lastly, collectivism arises logically from classical liberalism out of sheer necessity. Having shorn human ties to the vast web of intermediating institutions that sustained people through good and bad times, the expansion of the experience of individualism renders humans bereft of recourse to those traditional places of support and sustenance. The more individuated the polity, the more likely that a mass of individuals will inevitably turn to the State for help in times of need. This observation—made before Nisbet most powerfully by Tocqueville—suggests that individualism is not the alternative to Statism, but its very cause. As Tocqueville wrote late in *Democracy in America,*

> "Since . . . no one is obliged to lend his force to those like him and no one has the right to expect great support from those like him, each [person] is at once independent and weak. These two states—which must neither be viewed separately nor confused—give the citizen of democracies very contrary instincts. His independence fills him with confidence and pride among his equals, and his debility makes him feel, from time to time, the need of the outside help that he cannot expect from any of them, since they are all impotent and cold. In this extremity, he naturally turns his regard to the immense being [the tutelary, bureaucratic, centralized State] that rises alone in the midst of universal debasement. His needs and above all his desires constantly lead him back toward it, and in the end he views it as the unique and necessary support for his individual weakness."[2]

Far from fundamentally opposing one another, the individualism arising from the philosophy of classical liberalism and the subsequent philosophy of collectivism have been mutually reinforcing. Indeed, they have powerfully combined to all but rout the vestiges of the ancient conception of virtue as a practice or even an option. Today's classical liberals and progressive liberals remain locked in a battle for their preferred endgame—whether we will be a society of ever more perfectly liberated, autonomous individuals or ever more egalitarian members of the global "community," but while this debate continues apace, the two sides agree on essential means to achieve their distinct ends, thus combining in a pincer movement to destroy the vestiges of the classical practices and virtues that they both despise.

2   Alexis de Tocqueville, *Democracy in America,* II.iv.3, 644.

To the extent that modern "conservatism" has embraced the arguments of classical liberalism, the actions and policies of its political actors have never failed to actively undermine those areas of life that "conservatives" claim to seek to defend. Partly this is due to drift, but more worryingly, it is due to the increasingly singular embrace by many contemporary Americans—whether liberal or "conservative"—of a modern definition of liberty that consists of doing as one likes through the conquest of nature, rather than the achievement of self-governance within the limits of our nature and the natural world. Unless we recover a different, older, and better definition and language of liberty, our future is more likely than not to be one not of final liberation of the individual, but our accustomed and deeply pernicious oscillation between the atomization of our Lockean individualism and the cry to be taken care of by the only entity that is left standing in the liberal settlement, the State. If we care about liberty, we need rather to attend to our states and localities, our communities and neighborhoods, our families and churches, making them viable alternatives and counterpoints to the monopolization of individual and State in our time, and thus to relearn the ancient virtue of self-government.

This chapter began yet again as a lecture that was delivered to a group of bright students at a summer Honors program sponsored by the Intercollegiate Studies Institute, held during July of 2011. The topic of that program was "The Language of Liberty."

Chapter 10
Choosing the Road to Serfdom

It is worth calling to mind two commercials that aired at different times in the recent years. The first aired in 2010, and was produced by the Census Bureau in an effort to encourage Americans to fill out their census forms. It showed a somewhat slovenly man sitting in his living room dressed in a bathrobe, who talks directly into the camera in order to tell viewers that they should fill out the census form, as he's doing from his vantage as a couch potato. Fill out the census, he says, so that you can help your neighbors—and at this point he gets out his chair and walks out the front door, past his yard and the white picket fence and points to his neighbors who are getting into their car—"You can help Mr. Griffith with better roads for his daily car pool commute," he says—and then, indicating the kids next door, "and Pete and Jen for a better school," and continues walking down the street. Now neighbors are streaming into the quaint neighborhood street, and he tells us that by filling out the census, we can help Reesa with her healthcare (she's being wheeled by in a gurney, about to give birth), and a pair of elderly neighbors with their retirement, and so on and so on . . . "Fill out and send in your census form," he screams from a middle of a crowded street, "so that we can all get our fair share of funding, and you can make your town a better place!"

The other ad, produced in 2012, was produced by the Committee to Re-Elect the President—Obama—though it was not aired on television and has today altogether disappeared from the internet. It was entitled "The Life of Julia," and in a series of slides, it purported to show how government programs had supported a woman named Julia at every point in her life, from pre-school funds at a young age to college loans to assistance for a start-up to healthcare and finally retirement. In contrast to the Census commercial—which portrayed a neighborhood street filled with people who knew each other's names—"The Life of Julia" portrayed a woman who appeared to exist without any human ties or relationships, except—in one poignant slide—a child that had suddenly appeared but who was about to be taken away on a little yellow school bus, and as far as we're shown, is never seen again. No parents, no husband, a child who disappears.

The first ad is a kind of Potemkin Village behind which is the second ad. The first ad shows a thriving community in which everyone knows each other's names, and as you watch it—if you aren't duped by what it's portraying—you are left wondering *why in the world would we need government to take care of our neighbors if we knew each other so well? Why is my obligation to these neighbors best fulfilled by filling out the Census form?* The commercial is appealing to our cooperative nature and our sense of strong community ties to encourage us to fill out the Census form, but in fact in order—as the commercial tells us—to relieve us of the responsibility of taking care of each other, or perhaps more accurately, reflecting a world in which increasingly we *don't* know our neighbors' names, and instead turn to the government for assistance in times of need.

The second commercial is what lies "behind" the Potemkin village of the first. Julia achieves her "independence" by means of her reliance upon the government. Her life is a story of "success" because she has been supported at every step by a caretaker government. She has been liberated to be the person she wants to become by virtue of being the beneficiary of the government dime. Julia, in fact, is *freed of the bonds that are portrayed in the Census commercial.* Freedom is where there are no people—only Julia and the government.

The title of this 50th meeting of The Philadelphia Society is "The Road Ahead—Serfdom or Liberty?" I heard the word liberty often in many of the speeches throughout the weekend and saw it in the materials included in the conference packet and the 50th anniversary retrospective But here's the problem: I think Julia regards her condition as one of *liberty*. She is free—free to become the person that she wanted to become, liberated from any ties that might have held her back, whether obligations to take care of aging parents or (apparently) to live with a husband, or relying on someone to help her with a business, or with her care as she grew old. Would she call her condition "Serfdom"? Serfdom, to be accurate, is an arrangement whereby you owe specific duties to a specific person, a Lord—and in turn, that Lord owes you specific duties as well. What the life of Julia portrays is, in a strictly factual sense, the polar opposite of Serfdom—it portrays the life of a human being for the first time in human history who is FREE from any specific bonds or obligations to anyone (except maybe to her child until she gets him on the little yellow bus). If you were to ask Julia what she would prefer—Serfdom or Liberty—she would surely respond Liberty.

But it's a particular kind of liberty—a liberty unaccompanied by concrete duties and responsibilities to one another, but rather, abstract relationships increasingly and ever-more comprehensively mediated through the State. Because for Julia, and the denizen of the modern liberal state, our truest liberty is achieved when it is uniformly and unfailingly provisioned by the State, and not on the unreliability of any other set of relations or institutions. This was the main point of E. J. Dionne's latest book, *Our Divided Political Heart*, who argued that "community" and the State were the same thing, and the point summed up in a line stated several times during the Democratic National Convention, "The government is the only thing we all belong to."

And this was exactly what early conservative thinkers recognized was the "end-game" of liberalism—it sought, to the greatest extent possible, the elimination of all constitutive ties to any mediating or civil institution to be replaced by our direct relationship with the State. This would be accomplished not by means of enslaving the population, but by promising that this constituted the very essence of liberation. This was the basic insight of Tocqueville's culminating chapters of *Democracy in America*—that the democratic despotism of a mild "tutelary" state would come about not by force and terror, but by the willing acquiescence of an isolated and individuated citizenry. This was the argument of Bertrand de Jouvenel, who observed in his neglected masterpiece *On Power* that the rise of the centralized modern State came about when monarchs, seeking to break the power of local lords, promised liberation to the people in return for their direct fealty, and thus began a long and familiar tradition of expanding State power in the very name of liberation of individuals from mediating ties. His argument was refined and made with distinct power in the modern context by Robert Nisbet in the earliest years of American conservatism, in his 1953 book *Quest for Community*, where he argued that totalitarianism was not simply the imposition of despotic force upon a recalcitrant people—it was never that—but *desired* by populations whose "longing for community" had been transferred from a range of identities and memberships below the level of the State, to the State itself.

We begin to see this with ever-growing clarity in our own times—a new, kinder and gentler totalitarianism. It promises its citizenry liberty at every turn, and that liberty involves ever-greater freedom from the partial institutions of civil society, or ones remade in accordance with the aims of the State. As Wall Street Journal columnist Daniel Henninger pointed out in a recent lecture, the States as sovereign political units have been almost wholly eviscerated, and are now largely administrative units for the federal government. Satisfied with that victory, we now see extraordinary efforts to "break" two institutions that have always been most resistant to totalitarianism: churches and family. We see an unprecedented effort by the federal government to abridge religious liberty by conscripting religious institutions like Little Sisters of the Poor to be the agents providing abortifacients, sterilization and contraception—in the name of individual liberty. We can expect determined and even ferocious efforts to bend churches to accept gay marriage as a norm, even to the point of forcing them entirely out of the civil realm (as was done with Catholic adoptions in Massachusetts). And we see increasing efforts by the government to "liberate" children from their families—represented perhaps most chillingly by the MSNBC clip showing Melissa Harris-Perry explaining how the greatest obstacle to State education has been the pervasive notion that kids "belong" to families rather than belonging "collectively to all of us."

This broader social, cultural, political, and economic pedagogy is having extraordinary success. A recent Pew study on the behavior and beliefs of the "Millennial" generation—those 18 to 32 years old—suggests that this is the least connected, most individualistic and therefore "freest" generation in American history. In comparison to previous generations at a similar point in life, they are least likely to belong to a political party, least likely to be members of a church, least likely to be married by age 32. They have high levels of mistrust, yet strongly identify as liberals and support President Obama. These are the generation whose best and brightest occupied the administration building recently at Dartmouth, demanding "body and gender self-determination"—among other things, that sex-change operations be covered on campus insurance plans. They are a generation that is increasingly formed by a notion of autonomy as the absence of any particular ties or limiting bonds—and while they highly mistrust most institutions and relationships, they nevertheless view the government as a benign source of support for their autonomy.

So, as I look again at the program title, I must admit that it's not obvious to me what I'm supposed to favor—The Road to Liberty or Serfdom? Because, as thinkers like Nisbet recognized at the very beginning of the conservative movement in America, the rise of individual autonomy and centralized power would grow together—Leviathan would expand in the name of liberty. He understood that the most fundamental obstacle to the rise and expansion of the State was the "little platoons" praised by Edmund Burke particular and real ties to private, religious and civil institutions. He called for a "new laissez faire"—a laissez-faire of groups. He understood that what would prevent the rise of the kind of Liberty promised by Leviathan would be something like a robust patchwork of more local institutions and relationships that gives at least this nod to one aspect of "serfdom"—debts and gratitude to each other. Obligations and responsibilities should and must be grounded in real human relationships. Now, I'm not proposing that our rallying cry should be, "Give me Serfdom or give me death!" I don't think pushing serfdom is going to make conservatives more popular today. But I do think we need to recognize that conservatives haven't cornered the market in promoting "liberty," and if that is our totem, then the Progressives will win the debate, as on many fronts they are doing today. What distinguishes Conservatism is not that it believes merely in liberty – understood as autonomy—but that it has always understood that liberty is the necessary but not sufficient condition for living a human life in families, communities, religious institutions, and a whole range of relationships that encourage us to practice the arts of self-governance.

This panel asks us to consider "the road ahead" in the realms of economics, culture, and politics. For the central vision of Conservatism to survive the coming storm, in all these realms it must provide a better and fuller understanding of liberty, liberty as self-rule learned and practiced amid robust human relationships and personal bonds of trust and shared sacrifice. Conservatives just can't be *against* Progressivism, because increasingly that is seen by the world as being against the freedom of everyone to do anything. In the realms of economics, politics and culture, it must turn creatively to promoting ideas, policies and ways of living that show, support, and protect the excellence of the life, not of Julia, but of families, communities, churches, and institutions that have always been the schoolhouses of republican self-government.

These are the prepared remarks for a lecture I was invited to deliver at the 50ᵗʰ annual meeting of The Philadelphia Society in Chicago, IL. The theme of the meeting was "The Road Ahead: Serfdom or Liberty?" In my remarks, I sought to make the case that serfdom (properly understood) had some appeal, in contrast to liberty (improperly understood) as license. While I don't think many in my audience were moved to advocate for a return to medieval political arrangements, the lecture's basic argument was well-received.

Chapter 11
The Future of Democracy in America

I. Two Kinds of Liberty

Let me begin at the beginning—with Aristotle, of course. In Book 6 of his great work, *The Politics*, we find the only time he describes the principle of democracy to be liberty, and provides two understandings of *liberty* by which democracies can be guided. The first way in which liberty can be manifested in democracy echoes Aristotle's consistent definition of citizenship, which he describes numerous times in *The Politics* as "ruling and being ruled in turn." By this definition, liberty is a form of self-rule, the sharing in rule by citizens in which one is ruled by laws that are self-made. This is a special definition of liberty, calling upon the widespread presence of virtues that are required by self-government, including moderation, prudence, and justice. To "rule and be ruled in turn" is also to live in understanding of Aristotle's great and hard teaching, that "man is by nature a political animal," that we are only fully human when we live in political communities in which we learn to govern our basest impulses and aspire to attain our human telos, our end, to the greatest extent possible. By this definition, democracy is the most idealistic regime of all, the one that aspires to the greatest possible extension of virtue to all citizens; but, by this same definition, it is also the most demanding and perhaps least achievable, since it requires a special set of circumstances, above all a special kind of schooling in citizenship, that permit the widespread flourishing of the art and practice of self-government.

The other way in which the principle of liberty manifests itself is what Aristotle describes as the ability "to live as one likes," for he notes that some democrats say that it is preferable "to be ruled by none, or if this is impossible, to be ruled and rule in turn." Outwardly this form of liberty can look the same as the first version of democracy—for it involves the appearance of ruling and being ruled in turn. But its principle of liberty is not based upon the embrace of self-rule, especially citizenship, as the essence of liberty, but instead the acceptance of the appearance of rule as a second-best option. Aristotle describes a situation in which, by this second understanding of liberty, our deepest desire is to "live as one likes," which, for the ancients, is the very definition of tyranny. However, realizing that no one of us can achieve the condition of all-powerful tyrant, we agree instead to the second-best option of living under democratic forms. In such a condition, we outwardly exhibit the appearance of citizenship, but such democrats harbor a deeper desire to "live as one likes." Such democrats have the souls of tyrants.

Aristotle's distinction is worth keeping in mind, because today most democracies are liberal democracies, and thus, have the principle of liberty at their heart. However, liberal democracies are often content to fudge the difference between the two definitions, and often implicitly accept the second definition of liberty to be fundamental. America is a nation that is a perfect portrait of the tension between these two definitions. It was founded first by Puritans who articulated almost verbatim Aristotle's first definition of liberty. This was the founding of America so admired by Alexis de Tocqueville during his visit to the United States in the early 1800s, who in Chapter 2 of the first volume of *Democracy in America* quoted these lines from one of America's earliest Puritan intellectuals, Cotton Mather:

> I would not have you mistake your understanding of liberty. There is a liberty of corrupt nature, which is affected both by men and beasts, to do as they want. This liberty is inconsistent with authority and impatient of all restraint. This liberty is the grand enemy of truth and peace, and all the ordinances of God are bent against it. But there is another form of liberty, a civil, a moral, a federal liberty, which is the proper end of all authority. It is the liberty for that only which is just and

good, and for this idea of liberty you are to stand with the hazard of your very lives.[1]

Tocqueville noted that this understanding of liberty informed the practices of the citizens in the townships of New England, even long after the dissolution of the closed and confining Puritan communities of the 1600s. By the time Tocqueville visited America, he witnessed this kind of liberty—the practice of "ruling and being ruled in turn"—in vibrant forms of local self-governance throughout New England. He wrote that what he saw there was an admirable combination of "the spirit of liberty" and "the spirit of religion," one in which the spirit of liberty was moderated by the truth of our condition under God, and in which religion supported the practices of political liberty. Tocqueville admired especially the spirit of common good that pervaded the New England townships and the rich fabric of associations that populated civil society. He praised these forms of "local freedom" and especially the educative force of active civic engagement which, he wrote, drew people "from the midst of their individual interests, and from time to time, torn away from the sight of themselves." Through what he called "the arts of association," citizens were "brought closer to one another, despite the instincts that separate them, and brought them to aid each other." He called the local townships and associations "the great schools" of democracy, inculcating a spirit of healthy democratic orientation toward a common good. Through civic life—that ancient practice of "ruling and being ruled in turn"—Tocqueville observed that democratic citizens "learn to submit their will to that of all the others and to subordinate their particular efforts to the common action." Through the activity of political life, he wrote, "the heart is enlarged."

If America was founded according to a spirit of liberty that encouraged the practice of Aristotle's first understanding of democracy, centered especially on the practice of self-government among citizens, America also had a subsequent Founding in which the second understanding of liberty dominated. This is the Founding that drew especially

1   Alexis de Tocqueville, *Democracy in America*, trans. George Lawrence (New York: Harper Perennial Modern Classics, 2000), I.ii.2, 42.

upon the understanding of the social contract philosophy of John Locke, and informs the core documents of the American government such as the Declaration of Independence and the Constitution. According to Locke, by nature human beings are born free into a State of Nature in which law and government are absent. Our natural condition is one of complete freedom and lawlessness, and only in order to escape the "inconveniences" of the State of Nature do we form a contract and abridge our natural freedom. To live under government and law is a second-best option: the first best option would be for everyone else to abide by the terms of the social contract while I would be free to transgress against those terms. But, being informed by reason as well as constrained by law, we abide by the terms of the contract in spite of our inner desire to "live as we like."

By this Lockean understanding, government exists only to secure our rights and to advance our individual freedom. It does not seek to foster conditions in which our souls are educated in self-government, and thus Locke—following Hobbes—rejects the ancient idea that there is a summum bonum or a finis ultimus. We are authorized to define our own conception of the good (or to reject the idea of any such conception), and the role and purpose of government is to provide the conditions, as far as possible within the bounds of civil peace, that allow the full flourishing of individual freedom. Thus, while law is most fundamentally an unnatural imposition on our natural freedom, increasingly under such a government, the law will be increasingly oriented to expanding the sphere of personal liberty. Citizenship as a practice of self-rule is replaced by a definition of democracy dominated by a belief in personal freedom and autonomy. The only shared belief is that individual freedom should be expanded to the greatest extent possible, and government becomes charged with providing the conditions for that expansion.

Unsurprisingly, there is a tension if not outright contradiction between these two understandings of liberty. For the first, liberty to "live as one likes" is a contradiction to the idea of liberty in conformity with a conception of the human good. Its libertarian leanings, stressing the choices of individuals, proves destructive to the institutions and practices that are essential to an education in ordered liberty. The second understanding of liberty understands the first to be illiberal, based upon a conception of human good that confines the liberty of individuals to choose their own life-style. It demands liberation from the confines of restraining customs and laws, arguing that individuals should have the fullest freedom possible to chart their own life path. Yet, as contradictory as these two understandings of liberty are, they have both deeply informed the American self-understanding. They combined in a powerful coalition during the Cold War especially, presenting a common front against the collectivism and atheism of Communism, which they both opposed for different reasons. They have co-existed, if uneasily, for much of American history, perhaps in even salutary ways restraining the excesses of the one while correcting the other's deficiencies. But, much evidence today suggests that they are undergoing a long-term divorce.

II. The Great Divorce

What Tocqueville describes in *Democracy in America* is the co-existence of these two forms of liberty, but predicts a slow but steady advance of the second understanding of liberty—the "live as one likes"—in place of the first, "ruling and being ruled in turn." If he sees great evidence of civic practices in America of the 1830s, he also detects tendencies in democracy that will incline it, over the long term, toward an understanding of liberty in which people will seek to "live as they like." He predicts the rise of individualism and the decline of civic engagement and mutual responsibility for the fate of fellow citizens, and, as a consequence, foresees the rise of a centralizing State that will take on many of the functions and duties that would once have been part of local practice. Many recent studies of American civic life seem to confirm Tocqueville's prescient conclusions. Studies ranging from books such as Robert Bellah's *Habits of the Heart* to more recent books on civic participation and American religion by Robert Putnam confirm that Americans have become more individualistic and self-oriented over time. At the same time, Americans have become less prone to be engaged in the activities of civic life and regard such activities to be interferences on their individual freedom. By one measure then, we are "more democratic"—more free to pursue our individual ends. By another measure, we are less democratic, less apt not only to participate in civic life, but less willing to entertain the idea of a common good and to moderate our self-interest in the spirit of common weal. There are fewer and fewer informal spaces in which the civic art of "ruling and being ruled in turn" can be trained and exercised. And, as Aristotle would observe, without practice, civic virtues will atrophy and weaken.

Tocqueville also warned Americans that they are self-deceived if they believe that democracy can survive if it defines itself in an increasingly exclusive way as "living as one likes." Americans, he suggests, come to take for granted their inheritance of practices and institutions in which the civic arts can be learned and exercised. However, without consciously attending to their continuation, over time they will be weakened and abandoned in favor of individualism and "living as one likes." Today we see growing evidence of weakening relationships and ties throughout American society, from bonds of community and neighborhood to the ties of family life, to declining religious adherence. Many of those ties are today discarded or abandoned in the belief that they restrain individual freedom, but what is neglected is the way that their presence has been the necessary training ground on which the arts of civic self-rule were learned. Their abandonment—in the name of democratic freedom—today imperils democracy itself. In the name of individual freedom, we increasingly abandon the aspiration of self-rule.

For this reason, Americans must be confronted with a difficult question: is it possible that its victory in the Cold War over the great threat of Collectivism may yet prove to be a Pyrrhic victory, if it be the case that only two decades later we see growing signs that American society is no longer capable of self-government? Was the health of liberal democracy over-stated in comparison to its vicious twentieth-century ideological rivals, with its own inherent weaknesses today coming more fully into view? I believe the great challenges now facing the United States—economic, political, social and otherwise—are more than merely a passing crisis, but are manifestations of this deeper question whether a democracy based upon the ideal of "living as one likes" can survive. Evidence of the ruins of this belief are all around us. In our financial crisis we see the evidence of a set of behaviors in which greed and self-interest dominated a concern for the common weal. In our current debt crisis we see evidence of the way in which our obligations to future generations have been traded for today's comforts. In our growing partisan divide we see the expression of raw interest that neglects our greater civic obligation to seek out the common good. In our high levels of divorce and the practices of serial monogamy, we see evidence of a self-serving definition of our most central relationships. In our massive over-consumption of resources we see evidence of selfishness that neglects the consequences of our actions upon the globe and upon future generations. I could go on.

III. The Parties Today

What would fascinate Tocqueville the most about America today is not only the evidence of the truth of his predictions, but how there persists at least a residue of the older understanding that democracy requires us to "rule and be ruled in turn." In our two political parties we see evidence of both definitions of democracy, the ongoing presence of the internal contradiction that has been present in America from its earliest moments. In our Democratic Party—the party of President Obama—there are two simultaneous tendencies. There is, on the one hand, the belief that concerning lifestyle choices—especially regarding matters of human sexuality—there should be no limits upon personal and individual autonomy. This Party especially has become the party that defends nearly unlimited access to abortions, as well as advancing a re-definition of marriage away from its grounding upon the union of one man and one woman. This Party denounces and even ridicules arguments about the need to promote the traditional values that sustain family life and a culture of modesty and self-restraint. At the same time, this Party also calls for restraints upon the Market, arguing that free markets encourage the vices of greed, produce indefensible forms of inequality, and lead to the degradation of the environment. In a speech given in 2009 at Georgetown University, President Obama cited the gospel of Matthew, chapter 7, verses 24–28, calling for America and the globe to build the economy not upon sand, but upon rock that could withstand the rains and floods. When it comes to economics and the environment, the Democratic Party cites the Bible to encourage an embrace of morality, but in personal choices of lifestyle, the Bible's admonitions are regarded as irrelevant.

Alternatively, our Republican Party—which in recent elections took over the lower house of Congress—defends personal morality, particularly pertaining to family life and sexual matters. The Republican Party has opposed the license to obtain abortions without limit, and has tirelessly sought limitations upon its practice. For this reason, for many decades many Catholics switched their historic allegiance from the Democratic Party to the Republicans, though their vote has recently tended to be closely divided. The Republican Party has promoted policies that they argue support "family values," including encouraging the support of traditional marriage, encouraging the formation and maintenance of families, and seeking policies that favor a moralization of society. At the same time, they have tirelessly defended an unfettered free market system that places greed, acquisitiveness and materialism at the heart of its endeavors, that encourages hedonism and the sexualization of our popular culture, and which has produced titanic levels of material inequality in our nation.

I think it is fair to say that at the heart of each of these parties is a self-contradiction, an incoherence at least *in theory*. However, I would argue, too, that this contradiction has tended to be resolved *in practice* in favor of that form of liberty that promotes a culture of "living as one likes." While the Republicans have been successful in promoting a free market system, they have not been very successful in their encouragement of their program in "family values." And, while Democrats have been successful in advancing the cause of freedom in personal lifestyle choice, they have been less successful in advancing a moralization of the economic system. In each case, the "Lockean" part of their agenda has undermined the "Aristotelian" part of their platform. And, in practice, the Republican promotion of unbridled free markets has led to the undermining of family stability, while the Democratic promotion of unbridled personal freedom has encouraged a broader hedonism that informs our economic lives. To "live as we like" increasingly undermines the institutions and practices that train us to "rule and be ruled in turn."

On this point, I believe the ancient tradition as it has been transmitted into modernity—particularly through the auspices of the Catholic Church—can be of great assistance to the future of democracy in America and the world. For, at the end of the twentieth-century, Saint John

Paul II articulated the argument that the true choice facing the world was not between collectivism on the one hand, and radical individualism on the other, but between a true and false understanding of the human anthropology—human nature. This is a false dichotomy that Americans have come to accept over the years, even though neither party fully accepts the terms of the debate. America remains imperfectly a nation of Lockeans, tending as the years pass to dissolve the institutions and practices that chasten the tendency to "live as one likes" and promote the practice of "ruling and being ruled in turn," showing evidence of becoming more individualistic in our practice with each passing year. The future of democracy, in America and everywhere, depends on correcting this tendency toward a flawed definition of democracy, and re-learning the ancient art of "ruling and being ruled in turn."

This chapter was originally a lecture delivered at the Ignatianum Academy in Krakow, Poland, on May 25, 2011. I had taught a short course on American political thought, and rounded out my visit with this public lecture for a Polish audience interested in the fate of democracy in America—and Poland, and everywhere for that matter.

Chapter 12
After Liberalism

My title—"After Liberalism"—is an intentional play on Alasdair MacIntyre's landmark 1984 book, *After Virtue*. By the time we reach the conclusion of that book, we are to understand that to live "after virtue" is a fearful matter—one not unlike living on the cusp of a new Dark Ages, a time in which our main hope is to await a "new and doubtless very different St. Benedict," at least as MacIntyre famously concludes his book. And so, one might easily surmise that I am going to talk about an equally and possibly even more fearful condition, the state of the world we might imagine "after liberalism." And this would not be an unreasonable supposition, since the visible alternatives to liberalism on the world stage are genuinely fearful—from cruel tyrannies to crony dictatorships, from unstable democracies to newly aborning Islamist theocracies, from thugs in uniforms to mullahs in robes.

But I propose this theme not to warn of a terrifying political future and urge defense of liberalism to the last breath, but a better possibility that is, at this point, still difficult to imagine. What I want to try to outline in too few pages are reasons why we should actively *hope* for an end to liberalism, and seeking actively as thinkers, actors, citizens and—for many of us, Christians—a fourth sailing—after antiquity, after Christendom, after liberalism—into a post-liberal and hopeful future. But this inquiry and action will require prudence, imagination, creativity and patience, above all, the courage to recognize that what for many of us has been bequeathed to us as the last, best hope for political life is, in fact, not what we thought it was.

Liberalism is one of those words that mean many different things to different sets of ears, but what I will briefly outline tonight is that liberalism is not what we typically think it is. It is not constitutionalism, not the rule of law, not rule by elected representatives, not the separation of Church and State, not the recognition of rights attached to individuals. All of these features, and more we might name, are the inheritance of a pre-liberal tradition, developed especially throughout the period of Christendom that we moderns are often prone to label "the Dark Ages." Liberalism is a distinct way of thinking of these various institutional, legal, judicial and even social arrangements that now largely claims them all of its own making and invention.

Liberalism is the first and oldest of the world's great modern ideologies, and arguably the only remaining ideology following the demise of Fascism and Communism, in which it played such a determining role in defeating. By "ideology," I mean not simply a set of "ideas" about politics—as the word is promiscuously used today—but rather, a system of ideas that proposes a seamless political architecture, outside of which existing political arrangements are deemed to be illegitimate and require immediate remaking. This transformative instinct is the approach to politics that thinkers as various as Edmund Burke, Michael Oakeshott, Isaiah Berlin and Hannah Arendt criticized in their work rejecting the disfiguring role of modern ideologies. Today, it is widely accepted that Fascism and Communism are failed ideologies, justly relegated to the dustbin of history. It is not widely acknowledged, much less recognized, that Liberalism is equally an ideology, and only in some largely neglected corners, whether it is also fated, if not already deposited, in the same dustbin, for related reasons pertaining to its status as an ideology, albeit largely unaware of its own similar destination.

Largely unrecognized is that we generally operate within a paradigm that was famously articulated by Francis Fukuyama in 1991—that liberalism is the "end of history." Fukuyama argued that two main imperatives made liberalism the "end-station" for all political organizations, whether they were in fact at that point or not. These were two facts built into human beings and the nature of both political and human reality. The first of these was the universal requirement for advances in science and technology, particularly for military ends, but also related to economic development and prosperity, to both of which any political system must be strongly committed, and which liberal democracy best provides for given its arrangements promoting free inquiry and scientific advancement. The second of these was drawn less from the material than the "moral realm," a concept he derived from Hegel called "*annerkenung*," or "Recognition," but which we might also call "equal dignity." Here again, Fukuyama argued that liberal democracy uniquely affords all citizens equal recognition or dignity, premised as it is upon the equal membership and rights of every citizen, regardless of parentage, place of origin, wealth, occupation, race, ethnicity, gender, or any other feature that might be thought to distinguish people into wholly different political categories.

"The End of History" puts to rest what had been the longstanding undertaking of political philosophy—the debate over regimes. Whether in the realm of theory—in which the likes of Plato and Aristotle, Aquinas and Dante, Montesquieu and Tocqueville, debated over the merits of distinct "regimes" (e.g., monarchy vs. aristocracy vs. democracy and so forth)—or, in the realm of practice, in which the possibility of shifting from liberal democracy to Fascism or Socialism or Communism was a serious point of consideration by leading intellectuals until very recent times, entertaining the thought of alternative regime types was a leading form of political analysis. When I was just entering the profession of political science, it was striking that most colleges and universities had on the books a course in Marxism—which, during job interviews, I was often asked if I could teach, since the professor who had begun it was often either retiring or dead. Most of those courses have now entirely disappeared from the books, lacking not only faculty to teach them, but any demand from students who are focused on getting jobs within the capitalist system their parents once questioned.

Accepting liberalism as the entirety of our political horizon means that any shortcomings of liberalism are necessarily and inescapably treated as correctible aberrations from liberalism—and not as systemic problems endemic to it. Political scientists today study the problems of liberal society with the presumption that its deficiencies can always be fixed by mechanisms available within liberal democracy. For instance, if voter turnout is low, then it can be increased by discovering the root causes of low turnout (for instance, some studies show correlation between low exposure to civic education and levels of voting), and by redressing those causes. What political scientists generally don't consider is whether it's built into the nature of liberal democracy itself to foster privatism and disconnection of citizens from public affairs, something that Tocqueville worried was endemic to liberal democracies and which the authors of the *Federalist Papers* even admit is something of their ambition in the design of the Constitution.

A moment's reflection on Fukuyama's own thesis should reveal what is more than a theoretical contradiction at the heart of liberalism, if we were to accept his analysis. He presents two basic commitments that are central and definitive of liberal democracy—scientific and technological advancement and progress, on the one hand, and "recognition" or equal dignity, on the other. But it's clear that these two commitments are not necessarily compatible with each other, and accumulating evidence suggests that they are and will continue to become increasingly antithetical to one another. In contemporary times, advances in technology allow us to extend life and comfort to many in our society who are deemed worthy of recognition, but also to eliminate many who are not, such as the unwanted unborn—particularly those who are diagnosed in the womb with genetic disorders like Down's syndrome, in which cases the abortion rate is now above 90%—and, increasingly, the elderly. And current trends suggest that advances in bio- and nanotechnology will begin to allow some humans with means to "enhance," through the selection of certain genetic advantages, gene splicing, introduction of bio-technology into the human body, and so forth. The Princeton molecular biologist Lee Silver concludes his book on this subject, entitled *Remaking Eden*, with a futurist vision in which two distinct humanities will arise—the "enhanced," who can afford to offer their children ever-more advanced forms of "enhancement," and the "unenhanced"—the children of those without means, or those with religious scruples about "remaking Eden." The self-created race, he suggests, will justly rule over those content with, or unable to correct, God's deficient gifts.

Now this might seem to be a concern born of science fiction, but I think this tension reflects a feature endemic to liberalism that Fukuyama does not explore or note. The "Hegelian" concept of *annerkenung* understates the way that "recognition" is to be achieved within the liberal paradigm. Liberalism is perhaps best defined as the effort to liberate individuals from all forms of arbitrary and non-chosen relationships. It places a priority upon the free and unencumbered choice of individuals to wholly shape their own lives through the accumulation of their own choices. This ideal is perhaps most pristinely captured in the image of the "Social Contract," by which unencumbered individuals, existing in a state of freedom and equality, voluntarily choose to agree to the creation of the political order that comes into being to protect their individual rights. But this ideal is laced throughout in ways that go well beyond politics. John Locke, for instance, describes the condition of children to their parents—once they have reached the age of maturity—as a condition akin to the "state of nature," in which they "choose what society they will join themselves to, what common-wealth they will put themselves under." The people whom they will associate with, even the polity they will join, is a matter of entirely free choice. Similarly, regarding religion, Locke's understanding of religious membership is thoroughly voluntarist. In his "Letter Concerning Toleration," he defines a church as "a free and voluntary society. No body is born a Member of any Church. Otherwise, the Religion of Parents would descend unto Children, by the same right of Inheritance . . . ." And a later liberal lion, John Stuart Mill, would condemn the "tyranny of custom" and argue instead that liberty must be protected to encourage "experiments of living" that would be the engine of a dynamic and progressing society.

This freedom to make yourself is the reason that government comes into existence, according to the chief architect of the American Constitution, James Madison. "The first object of government," writes Madison in Federalist 10, "is the protection of the diversity in the faculties of men"—that is, our different proclivities, abilities, interests, talents, dispositions—from which, he continues, "the rights of property originate." The political order exists to permit, even positively encourage, humans to differentiate themselves by their choices with near-infinite variety, unfettered by limitations of family circumstance, geographic accident, undesired citizenship, unwanted religious identity, and increasingly— we see—even gender or any other form of identity that would suggest some form of external limitation on our shaping of selfhood. Notably, Madison notes that it is from these forms of "diversity" that the "rights of property" originate: the differences of who we are and what we make of ourselves extend into the world, in our various capacities to achieve or propensity to fail, to create, to succeed. Government, then, exists to protect not only our natural and chosen differences, but the manifestation of those differences in differences in property.

Here Madison closely follows John Locke, who explains in his fifth chapter of *The Second Treatise on Government* that property rights arise when the invention of money for the first time allows real distinctions in humans to arise. Humans in the State of Nature are equal because there's really no subsistence—Locke compares the condition to the state of the newly-discovered Indians in the Americas—and so real differences between humans that might allow for economic differentiation cannot become salient. But with the invention of money, Locke writes, people can begin to accumulate beyond mere subsistence and it becomes evident that there are two kinds of people—"the industrious and rational," on the one hand, and "the querulous and contentious" on the other.

Inequality has always existed—the "poor are always with us," Christ acknowledged. But liberalism was advanced to perfect a rational system of inequality in which the "rational and industrious" would be rewarded for their achievements that could only come fully into fruition by minimizing any forms of deeply grounded social association or relationship. This system required dislodging people from a lived experience of embeddedness in family, culture, place and tradition. Liberalism, as the name suggests, sought to liberate people from all the institutions and relationships that—in the view of liberal thinkers—had held people back from achieving the fullness of their potential, and thereby benefitting society through their inventiveness and creativity. They argued for the diminution of membership to a form of marketplace choice that individuals could enter and exit at will, reserving always their options for future revision—where they would live, what they would do, whom they would marry—or not—who they would *be*. This empowered the "rational and industrious" while exposing the "querulous and contentious." The structure of society was rearranged to standardize, rationalize, and universalize this arrangement, and the liberal State became a guarantor of this rearrangement, from everything to supporting "internal improvements" (infrastructure) to promoting a national and then global marketplace, and from subsidizing America's automobile culture to forced provision of birth control. The nineteenth century's heavy progressive hand of eugenics policy had been disgraced by the encounter with National

Socialism, but a rationalized effort at empowering the strong has remained at the heart of liberalism from its very outset.

Today many are apt to conclude that growing evidence of "income inequality" or the division of the nation (and, the world), into ever-more perfectly sifted "winners" and "losers" is a *mistake* or departure from liberalism that liberalism can fix. "Progressive" liberals—often educated at elite institutions of higher education that have become one of the main institutional conduits for the sifting of the winners from the losers—bemoan the inequality, even as they flock to one of a half-dozen cities of the world where they live at a great divide from those who have lost in the meritocratic sweepstakes, and live lives that have far more in common with their elite "conservative" political opponents (classical liberals) than with those whose lot they pity, but in no way seek to share.

Those with eyes to see can recognize that this continual aborning world, coming daily more fully into view, is not a departure of or deviation from the liberal project, but its culmination. It is, quite possibly, the end of history, at least as far as the eye can see. Its end-game has a muse, an economist no less—Tyler Cowen, whose recent book *Average is Over* should be required reading of every American interested in the fate of the nation. His book argues that we are exiting a unique period in American history when we believed that there could be relative equality and relative social cohesion, to one in which we will effectively see the creation of two separate nations. Here is what he writes in his book's concluding chapter, entitled "A New Social Contract?":

> The forces outlined in this book, especially for labor markets, will require a rewriting of the social contract . . . . We will move from a society based on the pretense that everyone is given an okay standard of living to a society in which people are expected to fend for themselves much more than they do now. I imagine a world where, say 10 to 15 percent of the citizenry is extremely wealthy and has fantastically comfortable and stimulating lives, the equivalent of current-day millionaires, albeit with better health care.
>
> Much of the rest of the country will have stagnant or maybe even falling wages in dollar terms, but a lot more

opportunities for cheap fun and cheap education. Many of these people will . . . benefit from all the free or near-free services modern technology has made available. Others will fall by the wayside.

This framing of income inequality in meritocratic terms will prove self-reinforcing. Worthy individuals will in fact rise from poverty on a regular basis, and that will make it easier to ignore those who are left behind.[1]

Cowen predicts, based on current settlement trends, that this large portion of the population will settle in places that are, or come to look a lot like, Texas: cheap housing, some job creation, and sub-par government services. He suggests that political leaders today should consider erecting entire cityscapes of *favelas* in which low rent and free internet would be the draw, thus allowing a virtual world of distraction from the grim poverty and spiritual desiccation that will become a permanent way of life for most of our fellow citizens. Cowen ends his book on this hopeful note: "We might even look ahead to a time when the cheap or free fun is so plentiful that it will feel a bit like Karl Marx's communist utopia, albeit brought on by capitalism. That is the real light at the end of the tunnel."[2]

Cowen at one point entertains the question whether this scenario will be likely to bring on the "end of liberalism," and suggests that while it will cause some considerable political tensions and dislocation, we can ultimately expect a time of acquiescence and peace (I suppose this is where free virtual distractions come in). But in another sense, it will bring about the "end of liberalism" as I have been describing it—liberalism's culmination. We will have sorted the "industrious and rational" from the "querulous and contentious" with near-perfect precision. Unmentioned by Cowen is the likelihood that developments in genetic and bio- technology will further differentiate these two nations into what could potentially be two different humanities. It will be the "end of liberalism" as far as the eye can see.

1   Tyler Cowen, *Average is Over: Powering America Past the Age of the Great Stagnation* (New York: Dutton Books, 2013), 258.
2   Tyler Cowen, *Average is Over*, 258.

But my lecture title indicated that I would try to imagine a "humane post-liberal" world, which is admittedly difficult to conceive, given the power and extent of the forces now arrayed to realize this outcome. Nearly every human institution has been re-formed in the effort to realize this denouement, from political to educational to economic, with even a number of highly visible churches urging people to understand that the Gospel's main teaching is to help us to become wealthy. We seem to be trapped in Weber's iron cage, with little viable alternative, and I don't want to sugar-coat the challenge. But, if we are truly free beings, then our fate is not inevitable, and the first task then lies in recommending a different course, should this outcome not be one that most of us would truly desire.

Let's go back to the origins of liberalism, which understood inherited relationships, bonds, duties and memberships to be obstructions to the realization of our true selves. By another kind of telling, however, the existence of this world of thick relationships *was* what constituted our true selves, selves that are by definition in deep, interpenetrating relationships with others within longstanding forms of human organization. By another kind of telling, human life ought to be organized in such a way as a constant recollection that we are not merely selves that ought primarily to seek our own ends. By another kind of telling, a world of relationships, associations, and social structures existed not simply to "hold back" the strong, but in fact to protect the weak from the illusions of mastery by the strong. This was the sentiment expressed in one of America's oldest founding documents—not the *Declaration* or the *Constitution*, but a sermon delivered to emigrating pilgrims on the Arbella by John Winthrop, entitled "A Model of Christian Charity" (much quoted, seldom read).

In contrast to John Locke, who argues that we *begin* in the state of nature as equals and, through the contrivances of politics, economics and social arrangements that liberate us from our constitutive bonds to others, we are freed to become radically unequal, Winthrop begins his sermon by noting the inescapable inequality of human beings in all times and all places: "God almighty in His most holy and wise providence hath so disposed of the condition of mankind, as in all times some must be rich, some poor, some high and eminent in power and dignity, others mean and in subjection." God arranges the world like this *not* as an arbitrary punishment upon those poor and in subjection, but rather, as a visible sign that through our differences we are to perceive our mutual need and reliance upon one another: "[God creates us in this way] that every man might have need of other, and from hence they might all be knit more nearly together in the bond of brotherly affection. From hence it appears plainly that no man is made more honorable than another, or more wealthy, etc., out of any particular and singular respect to himself, but for the glory of his creator and the common good of the creature, man." For Winthrop, human society exists as a constant and ever-present reminder of this demanding discipline. The strong would be especially tempted to run roughshod over the weaker, which Winthrop argues requires the cultivation of a strong and deep sense of shared fate so "that the riche and mighty should not eate upp the poore . . ." In Winthrop's peroration he calls upon his fellow wayfarers to devote themselves to promoting the common good through the cultivation of a strong set of communal bonds.

> For this end, wee must be knitt together, in this worke, as one man. Wee must entertaine each other in brotherly affection. Wee must be willing to abridge ourselves of our superfluities, for the supply of other's necessities. Wee must uphold a familiar commerce together in all meekeness, gentlenes, patience and liberality. Wee must delight in eache other; make other's conditions our oune; rejoice together, mourne together, labour and suffer together, allwayes haueving before our eyes our commission and community in the worke, as members of the same body.

In the world that Cowen describes coming into being, we see the full flourishing of a different vision, in which to the greatest extent possible, our fates are disconnected, especially encouraged by the disassembling of the institutions and social forms that were devised to link the fates of the strong and the weak.

Today many of the communal forms of life that might once have been thought to link the fates of the strong and weak are attenuated or all but dissolved. There has been extraordinary geographic sorting, a result of extensive educational sorting (even President Obama sends his daughters to the exclusive Sidwell Friends School). We are engaged in the human equivalent of strip-mining, identifying "rational and industrious" young people in every city and town and hamlet through standardized testing, extracting them for processing at one of our refining centers (universities), and then excreting them now as productive units of economic production to be conveyed to a hub of economic activity while leaving behind a landscape stripped bare of talented and industrious people that God thought wise to distribute widely.

For a graduate of one of the institutions where I teach or where I have taught—Princeton, Georgetown, and Notre Dame—to return to one of these strip-mined places would be an indication of failure. How striking a contrast to the life led by one of my—and many Americans'—favorite Minnesotan, that transplanted son of Chisholm, Minnesota—Archibald Graham, better known as Archie "Moonlight" Graham of "Field of Dreams" fame. In spite of—or because—he held a medical degree, he spent fifty years in Chisholm, MN, where he served the children of the Chisholm schools and every Saturday could be found in his office offering free eye exams to poor children and giving away eyeglasses that he collected from townspeople. A scholarship in his name is still offered to two graduating seniors from the Chisholm High School. I dare say that were Doc Graham growing up today, he would have settled in one of five—or three—cities and there would be no scholarship named for him when he died. But he would make a lot more money than he probably made in little Chisholm. And every town in America had its Doc Grahams, but in the world described by Cowen, you can be damn sure that the future Doc Grahams will be extracted from the crowded *favelas*, never to be seen again.

I am not so unrealistic as to propose that an alternative to liberalism is a likely or even permissible prospect. But two things to me are clear: first, that as liberalism becomes more perfectly "itself," it will become more and more difficult to explain some of its endemic features as merely accidental or unintended. And, second, that in the face of this fact, alternatives will be sought, many of which will be no better and even worse. It is now the task for those with imagination and courage, and a deep commitment not only to humanity, but to human beings, to begin to envision an alternative future to the one to which we now seem destined, which will focus especially on beginning to put together what liberalism has torn asunder.

This chapter began life in the fall of 2014 as the annual Holmer Lecture at the University of Minnesota, sponsored by the campus Christian group MacLaurinCSF. I joined a list of impressive company—including Richard John Neuhaus, Stanley Hauerwas and Jean Bethke Elshtain— who had delivered previous Holmer Lectures. A large auditorium was quite full, and the audience was focused, intent, and keenly interested. The intensity of interest that evening helped persuade me that concerns about the prospects for liberal democracy were far from "merely academic"—they were gnawing anxieties that touched the heart of nearly every thinking citizen today. It was among the best-received lectures I can recall giving, and I was kept long afterwards in conversation with many members of the audience.

Index